100 Games & Activities for the Introductory Foreign Language Classroom

Thierry Boucquey, PhD
Karina Flores
Julia Kramer
Laura McPherson
Maggie Pettit
Hana Silverstein
Emily Tjuanakis

EYE ON EDUCATION
6 DEPOT WAY WEST, SUITE 106
LARCHMONT, NY 10538
(914) 833–0551
(914) 833–0761 fax
www.eyeoneducation.com

Library of Congress Cataloging-in-Publication Data

100 games and activities for the introductory foreign language classroom / Thierry Boucquey ... [et al.].
     p. cm.
   Includes index.
ISBN 1-59667-043-6
1. Languages, Modern—Study and teaching. I. Boucquey, Thierry. II. Title: One hundred games and activities for the introductory foreign language classroom.
   PB35.A14 2006
   418.0071—dc22

                     2006030463

10 9 8 7 6 5 4 3 2

Editorial and production services provided by
Richard H. Adin Freelance Editorial Services
52 Oakwood Blvd., Poughkeepsie, NY 12603-4112
(845-471-3566)

Also Available from EYE ON EDUCATION

Differentiated Instruction:
A Guide for Foreign Language Teachers
Deborah Blaz

Bringing the Standards
for Foreign Language Learning to Life
Deborah Blaz

A Collection of Performance Tasks and Rubrics:
Foreign Languages
Deborah Blaz

Foreign Language Teacher's Guide
to Active Learning
Deborah Blaz

Teaching Foreign Languages in the Block
Deborah Blaz

What Great Teachers Do Differently
14 Things That Matter Most
Todd Whitaker

Seven Simple Secrets:
What the Best Teachers Know and Do!
Annette Breaux and Todd Whitaker

Classroom Instruction from A to Z
How to Promote Student Learning
Barbara R. Blackburn

Classroom Motivation from A to Z
How to Engage Your Students in learning
Barbara R. Blackburn

Effective Schooling for English Language Learners:
What Elementary Principals Should Know and Do
Patricia Smiley and Trudy Salsberry

Acknowledgments

The authors wish to thank the Andrew W. Mellon Foundation, the generosity of which made possible the preparation of this volume. Its grant offered funding to support programs designed to increase faculty involvement in residential campus life and provided students with the opportunity to initiate and collaborate with faculty on compelling projects outside the classroom. The authors also wish to express their gratitude to Lori Kerns, principal at Chaparral Elementary School in Claremont, California, and her staff of dedicated teachers. Since the inception of the Chaparral-Scripps cooperative agreement in 1997, they have generously opened all their fourth- through sixth-grade classrooms for the Scripps College foreign language and culture student teachers. The fall 2005 semester enabled the authors to test and assess all the games and activities presented in this volume.

Table of Contents

Introduction

The purpose of this book is to be a resource for teachers who, more often than not, lack the time to create games for their classes or are simply looking for new and exciting ideas to enhance their teaching. The idea for this volume grew out of the Foreign Language and Culture Teaching Clinic class. It is one of the course options available to sophomores completing their third semester of the Core Humanities program at Scripps College in the Claremont University Consortium in California. The course explores the deep-rooted connection between language and culture in foreign language acquisition as well as the presentation of foreign languages and cultures in textbooks on the market. It offers approximately 20 young women the unique experience of teaching a foreign language in an elementary school classroom. Student teachers work in teams of two to teach third through sixth graders for 30 minutes twice a week. In the 8 years this course has been offered at Scripps, students have taught a broad range of languages, including Chinese, French, Spanish, German, Hindi, Japanese, and Korean. In its ninth year, Arabic and Persian will also be taught.

As one of the tenets of this class, teachers use the direct, or natural, method so that all instruction from day one is conducted in the target language. A typical class starts with a 15-minute expository dialogue, skit, or question-and-answer period, during which the children learn new vocabulary and/or grammar in an interactive, communicative way. Next, a 15-minute game or activity helps practice the new material presented. A collection of the latter has been compiled in this volume.

The resources offered in this book are appropriate and effective teaching tools, because all the games and activities have been laboratory tested in the fall of 2005 by the Scripps College Teaching Clinic class. Only the most successful have been retained for inclusion in this book and for use in your classroom.

Research has shown that games and activities provide a fun and interactive learning environment and are particularly conducive to effective language learning. When students are active, engaged, and enjoying themselves, their retention of new vocabulary and other linguistic functions is much higher than if they were simply learning by rote or performing drills. Many games described in this book involve total physical response (TPR), a teaching technique developed by James Asher in *Learning Another Language Through Actions* that uses body movements to attach concrete meaning to language.

Equally important and valuable is the creation of an imaginative, virtual yet realistic *foreign* atmosphere in the classroom to provide an abundance of stimuli, immersing the students in the target language and culture. Language learners should have the vivid impression of stepping into their target-language realm when they enter their classroom, one that is lively, multifaceted, and intriguing. You could accomplish this by, for example, setting up a traditional marketplace in the classroom, guiding the students on an imaginary train tour of the target country, dressing in traditional garb, and arranging a target-culture *corner* in your classroom. These experiences bring vocabulary to life and open the door to another culture.

The activities in this book are organized according to general themes such as weather, colors, telling time, or animals. Most of the themed sections are not language-specific; however, one section contains target-culture games designed to be taught in particular languages. For example, a few of the target-culture games pertain to Japanese origami or calligraphy. All the games in the other sections are applicable to a much broader range of languages and subjects. You can, for example, use the game "Hot and Cold" to teach about weather, pirates, or clothing in virtually any language.

Within each themed section, the objectives of the individual games are laid out, highlighting the specific skills or vocabulary each aims to teach. All the games include detailed playing instructions, a list of required materials, and any necessary guidelines for making the materials. Some games include helpful charts, worksheets, or other visuals. Others offer an account of the writer's experience playing the game with the class, and some describe optional but equally fun variations on games. The activities in the book are also cross-referenced in the index by topic, objective, and grammatical or linguistic pattern to facilitate the quick location of relevant material.

Teachers at the middle school, high school, and college levels need not assume that the activities in this book are limited to the elementary classroom. Most games and activities in this collection are applicable to any beginning language classroom and can be easily adapted to more advanced levels if needed. *100 Games and Activities for the Introductory Foreign Language Classroom* encourages the reader to draw on these games to produce stimulating, effective, and successful teaching in the target language and culture.

Scripps College
Claremont University Consortium
California
August 2006

1
Animals
and Their Habitats

Animal Collage

Topic
- Animals and their habitats
- Verb *to be (from)*

Materials
- Plain white paper (1 sheet per student)
- crayons, pens, or markers
- A few large poster sketches of different animal habitats (rainforest, ocean, desert, forest, house, etc.)
- Tape

Objectives
To reinforce animal and habitat vocabulary through art while incorporating the verbs *to be (from)* or *to live (in)*

Instructions
Pass out pieces of plain white paper to the students. Ask them each to make a simple drawing of an animal, choosing from the animals they have studied in class. When the students are finished with their drawings, students individually come to the front of the room, hold up their drawings, and announce their animals and the habitats in which they live. For example, to use the verb *to be (from)*, the student holds up the drawing of a frog and say, "The frog *is from* the rainforest." After announcing this, the students tape their animals on the appropriate habitat poster. Continue until all the animals are in their appropriate habitats, creating a beautiful animal collage that can be displayed in the classroom or disassembled so the students can keep their animal drawings and label them.

Note
If there is not enough time for students to come up individually, call them up by habitat. For example, say, "All the animals of the ocean come to the front." Then the students can still announce their animals but save time by not announcing the habitats.

Jungle Safari

Topic

♦ Animals

Materials

♦ Pictures of approximately five jungle animals

Objective

To learn about jungle animals

Instructions

Before class, tape the pictures in various places in the classroom. You are the tour guide and the students are tourists on this jungle safari. Lead them carefully around the room, as if stepping over vines and around trees, while the students try to spot the animals taped up around the room. Whenever they find a picture, the group circles it and repeats the animal's name, making the total physical response (TPR) noises and associated movements.

Note

This can also be a desert safari, a mountain trek, a farm visit, and so on, depending on the target culture.

Sounds on the Farm

Topic

◆ Farm Animals and Their Sounds

Materials

◆ Animal cards (1 per student)

Objectives

To reinforce the farm animal sounds specific to the target culture and use animal vocabulary

Instructions

To create the animal cards, draw or print out small images of the animals, with many on each page and multiple copies of each animal. Cut the page(s) of animals so that each *card* has one animal on it. The perceived sounds of farm animals vary between languages and regions. Search the Internet for any target culture's animal sounds that are unfamiliar.

After a lesson on farm animals and their sounds, pass out an animal card to each student. When the teacher asks, "What sounds do the farm animals make?" each student stands up and begins making the animal sound that corresponds to their animal. Students try to find their animal *family* by making their sound; for example, a chicken make its sound to find all the other chickens. When the animals have grouped into their families, the teacher tells the animals to stop making their sounds. The teacher asks each family one at a time, "What sound do you make? What animal are you?"

Examples

In our Spanish class, the students who received a rooster animal card made the sound, *quiri quiri quiri,* but each language had its own variation of the rooster sound: *cock-a-doodle-doo* (English), *cocorico* (French), *kokekokkoo* (Japanese), *kickeriki* (German), *kukru:ku:* (Hindi), *kukelekuu* (Flemish).

Note

Make sure the students keep their animal card hidden once they start making sounds so that they cannot cheat by showing it to the other students.

Trouble on the Animal Farm

Topic

+ Animals

Objective

To gain an understanding of the types of animals found within a country that speaks the target language

Instructions

Have the students sit in a circle. Modeling the game Duck-Duck-Goose, students play either the part of an escaped animal or the farmer trying to corral the animal back to the farm. Choose a student to begin the game by standing up and choosing an escaped animal to play. Next, have the remaining seated students in the circle make that animal's sound. After they have all made the sound, the *animal* begins to walk around the circle saying the animal name when touching a sitting student on the head. On reaching the student selected to be the *farmer*, the animal must then call out the name for farmer and make it back to the farmer's seat in the circle without being tagged by the farmer. The student playing the farmer could also be a zoo keeper, rancher, explorer, or similar persona depending on the types of animals most commonly found in the target country.

Example

In my Spanish class, we played Animal-Animal-Ranchero(a). Students took turns playing different farm animals and selecting a rancher who would try to *herd* them back to the farm.

2

Body Parts and Clothing

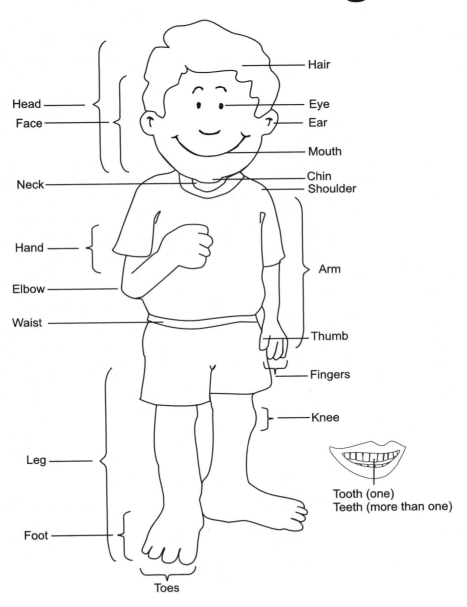

Hair

Head

Face

Eye

Ear

Mouth

Chin

Shoulder

Neck

Hand

Arm

Elbow

Waist

Thumb

Fingers

Knee

Leg

Tooth (one)
Teeth (more than one)

Foot

Toes

The Ambulance Ride

Topic
- Body parts
- Illnesses
- Verbs *to hurt* and *to break*

Materials
- 5 pictures of body parts or illnesses pasted or drawn on an index card

Objective
To practice using the words *to hurt* and *to break* in the context of illnesses and body parts

Instructions
Choose three to five student volunteers to act injured or sick. Each of the volunteers is secretly given a picture of the body part that is broken or hurting. The class then makes a circle around the *injured* students and take turns yelling to simulate an ambulance siren. After the *ambulance* sound has gone around once, ask it to stop. Point to an injured student and ask the class what they think is the problem as the sick student acts out the sickness or pain. The ambulance can only *pick up* a patient when someone has guessed the injury by shouting it out. The student who guesses the correct injury takes the classmate into the ambulance which means taking the injured student to the *hospital* outside the circle. The class should repeat the name of the injury once or twice for practice. Continue with a new injured student, until all the injured students have been picked up by the ambulance and have rejoined their classmates in the hospital.

Examples
In our Spanish class, our injured and sick students had a headache, stomachache, cold, broken leg, or broken arm.

Notes
You can make this activity into a competition by separating the class into two groups. The group that picks up its injured or sick students the fastest wins. Also, please be aware that this activity works best outside or in a big open space.

Body Bounce

Topic

- Body parts
- Numbers

Materials

- A medium-sized ball, such as a soccer ball, volley ball, or beach ball

Objective

To have the students practice numbers and names of body parts

Instructions

Have the students form a big circle. Go around the circle giving the ball to students to bounce on their knees. The class watches and says *knee* each time the ball hits the student's knees. When a student drops the ball, the next student tries the same, with the class repeating *knee* on each bounce. After a few students bouncing the ball on their knees, continue around the circle with students bouncing the ball on different body parts (head, hands, elbow, foot) and shouting the name of the body part on each bounce. If the students are enjoying the game, go around the circle again and ask, instead of instruct, the students, which body part they want to use.

Note

When practicing the word for *hand,* have the students bounce the ball on the back sides of their hands to make the task a bit more challenging.

Body Part Art

Topic

- ◆ Body parts
- ◆ Colors

Materials

- ◆ Coloring sheets (1 per student): copies of an artwork from the target culture that incorporates the human body; black and white line drawings work best so the students can easily identify and color the body parts
- ◆ 1 transparency copy of the coloring sheet (optional)
- ◆ 1 pack of crayons per student

Objectives

To test student knowledge of body part and colors vocabulary while experiencing art from the target culture

Instructions

Pass out a coloring sheet and pack of crayons to each student. Choose one volunteer at a time to announce a body part. For example, if the volunteer says, "Color the arms red," all the students color in the arms red. Continue until all body parts are colored in. After this process is finished, the activity can be enhanced by using a transparency copy of the coloring sheet and asking volunteers to come up and label the body parts. The students copy the vocabulary onto their own coloring sheet, which can be used as a study guide.

Examples

Our coloring sheets were copies of a Mexican Day of the Dead skeleton drawing.

Catwalk in the Classroom

Topic

- Clothing
- Fashion

Materials

- Various clothing items
- Stereo
- A compact disk with popular music from the target culture
- Stopwatch
- Two 15-foot strips of ribbon/rope or a 15' x 3' piece of paper/plastic to make a catwalk

Objective

To practice the names of everyday clothing items

Instructions

Separate the class into groups of five to seven students and tell them to choose three members of their group to be models. Put two big piles of clothing on the floor on opposite sides of the classroom. Choose two groups at a time to participate and designate them to a pile. Give the models 10 to 30 seconds to put on as many clothing items as they can. The students who are not models can help them put on clothes. When the time has passed, the models walk down the *runway*, and a group member who is not a model announces what they are wearing. Music should play while the students model to make the experience seem more authentic. The groups get 1 point for each clothing item worn that is correctly named. The group with the most points wins.

Note

It may be helpful to use popular music from target culture so that the students can model to it.

Middle School/High School Adaptation

Students prepare their outfits and speeches in advance.

Clothing Rubik's Cube

Topic

- ◆ Clothing
- ◆ Colors
- ◆ Verb *to have*

Materials

- ◆ Unisex paper dolls approximately 6 inches in height
- ◆ Clothing squares: black and white outlines of various clothing items set inside same-sized squares (approximately 1 × 1–inch squares for each item of clothing) that can be colored-in and easily cut out to dress the paper dolls

Objectives

To practice clothing and color vocabulary

Instructions

Give each student a paper doll and a sheet of paper showing at least four clothing squares. Instruct the students to color in each item of clothing using a different color they have learned. Next, have students cut out the squares and place them on their dolls. Then, ask each student to pick one color and write it on the back of their paper doll. This is the color they must try to find and from which they must make an entire outfit. Students must then walk around the classroom asking other students if they have various clothing items in that specific color, trading with their classmates to create an entirely monochromatic doll outfit. For example, a student who has chosen the color red goes around the room asking classmates, "Do you have red pants?" or "Do you have a red shirt?" until her paper doll is dressed entirely in red clothing squares. To add a competitive element, have the game end when a student successfully completes their monochromatic outfit, repeating the process as often as desired.

Here is an example of a set of four clothing squares. Students can choose what items to color in, as long as they use different colors for each item of clothing. Alternative squares could show a hat, socks, jacket, tank top, dress, or belt.

Note

If the game is played multiple times, have the students select a different color each time.

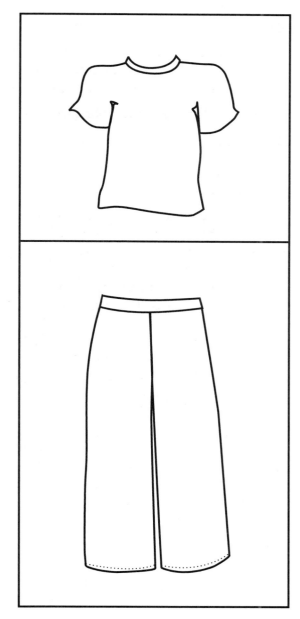

The Greatest Label Race of All Time

Topic

- Body parts

Materials

- Several sets of 3 × 5–inch note cards with different body parts written on them (at least eight cards per group, the number of sets of note cards depends on the size of the class)
- Tape to attach the note cards to the mannequin

Objective

To practice body part vocabulary

Instructions

Divide students into groups of five to eight depending on the size of the class. Then select a volunteer from each group to be the group's *mannequin*; the group places note cards on this student's body. Next, give each group identical sets of at least eight note cards with different body parts written on them, such as head, arm, hand, leg, foot, back, knee, elbow, shoulder, finger, and so on. Ask each group to place their note cards face down on a nearby table or the floor. When you give the signal, each group must hurry to correctly label its mannequin by taping the note cards to the body parts indicated on the cards. The first group to correctly label the mannequin wins. The game can be made more complicated by increasing the number or specificity of body parts, such as including the specific names for fingers or specifying right and left arms, legs, feet, or hands.

Notes

Avoid using any body parts that may make students feel uncomfortable such as chest or buttocks. If students might be uncomfortable acting as mannequins, large papers with blank outlines of the human body can be used instead.

Fashion Show

Topic

- Clothing
- Commands
- Verbs *to put on* and *to take off*

Materials

- 2 of each of the following clothing items: hat, pants, skirt, dress, shirt, jacket, and pairs of shoes, sandals, and socks

Objectives

To learn the commands *to put on* and *to take off* and the words for different articles of clothing

Instructions

Ask for a volunteer to come up and be the model. Then ask for other volunteers to tell the student what to put on over his or her own clothes. They must say the article of clothing as well as the correct command for *to put on*. The class repeats the name of the clothing article as the model puts it on. Keep calling on volunteers to give orders until the model is completely dressed. Then when the model takes off the clothes, the students repeats the names of the articles of clothing removed in unison. Repeat the game with a couple other models as time allows.

Notes

We wanted to avoid taking boys up to be models, because we knew the class would want them to wear skirts. However, like we imagined, the class demanded that a boy wear a skirt, and we consented. They got very giggly and excited about it; but we asked the boys if they were okay with it and gave them the option to wear pants, but they seemed eager to wear the skirts as well. The kids had a lot of fun in the end, and this was one of their favorite activities.

This game could also be made competitive. Divide the class into two teams. One student from each team races to put on one item of clothing after it is announced. Select another student to be the announcer. After the announcer yells out a clothing item, the two competitors race to find the item in their pile, put it on, and then yell out the name of the item. The first student to do this earns a point for the team and is the announcer for the next round. The game continues in this fashion. To make the game more advanced, the announcer could yell out a sequence of two or three clothing items. To win, the competitors must then put on the items in that order and yell out the names of the items in that order.

Hokey Pokey

Topic

♦ Body parts

Materials

♦ Translated version of the song, "Hokey Pokey" by Larry LePrise, 1950

Here is the English version:

You put your left foot in,	You put your right foot in,
you put your left foot out,	you put your right foot out,
you put your left foot in,	you put you right foot in
and shake it all about.	then you shake it all about.
You do the Hokey Pokey	You do the Hokey Pokey
and turn yourself around.	And turn yourself around.
That's what it's all about.	That's what it's all about.

The song is then continued with many different body parts.

Objective

To have the students practice the body parts.

Instructions

Have the students form a big circle. Teach them the "Hokey Pokey" song and have them sing it while going through the motions. Let the students shout out the body part they want to sing for the next verse.

Examples

Here is a Spanish version:

El pie izquierdo adentro.
El pie izquierdo afuera.
El pie izquierdo adentro.
Muévelo así.
La sofa papa pokey.
Date una vuelta.
Y esto es todo.

Continue with:

Los *codos* adentro…
La *cabeza* adentro…(*muévela así*)
El *pie* adentro…(*muevelo así*)
La *rodilla* adentro…
El *cuerpo* adentro…
La sofa papa pokey.
Date una vuelta.
Y esto es todo.

How to Pop

Topic

- ◆ Body parts
- ◆ Commands

Materials

- ◆ Balloons (enough for each group to have at least 10)
- ◆ Index cards cut in half with body parts drawn or written on them, enough to put one in each balloon

Objectives

To practice giving instructions with the verb *to use,* while reviewing the names of body parts

Instructions

Put the pictures of the body parts inside the balloons before inflating them. Split the class into three or four groups. Give each group five to ten balloons and tell them to stand in a circle with each member holding a balloon. Ask one student in each group to pop the balloon in any way. After the first balloon is popped, the student must use the picture of the body part to tell the next person in her group how the next balloon should be popped. That student must pop the balloon using the body part as directed. After popping the balloon, this student then uses the picture in the balloon to tell the next person how to pop the next balloon and continue the cycle. Students may not show the pictures to each other. They must tell each other how to pop the balloon to gain practice using the words. The first group to correctly pop all their balloons wins.

Here is a flow chart of order in which the balloons should be popped:
Student #1 (Pops in any way, gets paper, and tells Student #2 how to pop.) → Student #2 (Pops the way Student #1 instructed, gets paper, and tells Student #3 how to pop.) → Student #3 (Pops the way Student #2 instructed, gets paper, and tells Student #4 how to pop.) → Continue until the last student has popped.

Notes

Possible body parts include foot, hand, head, hip, stomach, thighs, or knees. Students can use a wall, floor, table, or chair to help them pop the balloon.

Human Symphony

Topic

♦ Body parts

Objective

To memorize the names of body parts in the target language

Instructions

Arrange the class so they are standing in a large circle outside or around the room. Introduce a first rhythm using the word for "hand," perhaps on straight quarter notes, clapping as everyone says the word. Practice this rhythm for a while, then stop and create an alternate rhythm with a different body part, such as "leg" on alternating quarter notes, slapping the leg as you say the word. Split the circle into two groups and layer the rhythms on top of each other. Keep adding more and more rhythms with different body parts until a complex "human symphony" has been created.

Example: Our Japanese class used five different body parts in the rhythms shown above. We introduced the first three, then slowly added the last two as the rhythms got more complicated. The more dance-like the movements, the more the students got into it.

In Your Suitcase

Topic

- ◆ Review
- ◆ Travel
- ◆ Clothing
- ◆ Numbers

Materials

- ◆ White sheets of paper for every student
- ◆ Colored pens, pencils, or crayons (enough for every student to use some)

Objectives

For the students to practice vocabulary associated with travel

Instructions

Pass out a sheet of white paper to every student. Once all of the students have their paper, tell them that the class is planning a trip to the target country and must prepare their suitcases for the trip. Then, generate a packing list on the board by asking students what they would put in their suitcases, for example: clothing, shoes, snacks, games, etc. Once the list has been generated, ask the students to draw on their sheet of paper a suitcase filled with items only they would bring. They may only choose from the items on the board.

After the students complete their suitcases, ask the class by a show of hands who has chosen to put which items in their suitcase. On the board, tally the number of students who chose to pack each item, noting the most popular ones.

Monster Parts

Topic

- Prepositions
- Body parts
- Animals
- Colors
- Numbers 1–10

Materials

- Blank paper
- Markers (enough for the class)

Objectives

For students to become familiar with prepositions, body parts, animals, and colors

Instructions

Before class, decide upon the body parts for a monster made out of the body parts of various animals to be dictated to the students. Dictate that monster to the students one body part at a time. Start with the head of the animal chosen earlier, then tell the students to draw the ears of the next animal on top of the head, the body of yet another animal below the head, the eyes of another animal inside of the head, etc. (See example below). When the whole monster is complete, either dictate which colors the body parts should be, or hand out a homework sheet with directions for coloring. Collect the drawings afterwards to ensure that the students properly understood the dictation.

Examples

"Draw a hamster's head. On top of the head, draw three rabbit's ears. Underneath the head, draw a cat's body. On the right and left of the body, draw turtles' arms. Beneath the body, draw two birds' legs. From behind the body, draw a fish's tail." We then handed out a set of directions for homework about the colors of the various body parts.

Note

You can also play this game in the following way: Split the class into groups (the number of students should match the number of body parts being dictated), and instruct each student to draw a head on her sheet of paper. Then tell the students to fold the paper over so just the bottom of the head is visible and pass the paper to the person next to them in their groups. Then give the instructions to draw shoulders and fold the paper over to the bottom of the shoulders. Continue passing, drawing, and folding like this until the students get their original papers back, at which point they can unfold them and see the strange person who was drawn.

Move It!

Topic

- ◆ Body parts
- ◆ Motions
- ◆ Speed

Materials

- ◆ 3 cups labeled *Body Cup, Speed Cup,* and *Movement Cup*
- ◆ *Body Cup:* Use at least 3 index cards and cut them in half. Paste small printed or drawn pictures of body parts on each. Fold each card and put them in the *Body Cup*
- ◆ *Speed Cup:* Cut 3 index cards in half and write the word "fast" or "slow" on each. Make 3 cards for each word. Fold them and put them in the *Speed Cup*
- ◆ *Movement Cup:* Use 3 index cards and cut them in half. Write a type of motion on each card. Fold them and put them in the third cup.

Objectives

For students to practice the names of body parts, motions, and speeds

Instructions

Ask for volunteers to come to the front of the class. Tell them to stand in a line facing the class. Ask each one individually to pick a paper from the *body cup,* the *movement cup,* and the *speed cup.* Each time a student picks from a cup, tell her to announce it to the class. After picking a body part, movement, and a speed at random, the student will have to use all three to make a motion for the class. For instance, if knees, circle, and fast are chosen, the student will have to move her knees fast in a circular motion.

Note

Possible body parts: head, neck, knees, feet, legs, hips, arms, hands, fingers, toes, etc. Possible movements: circular motion, triangular motion, shake, wiggle, etc.

Mystery Box

Topic

- Body parts
- Senses
- Review

Materials

- Three to five standard shoe sized boxes with a hand sized slot cut into the top of each box. Number every box so it can be identified later.
- Various items students can either smell, feel, taste, touch or see to be placed inside each box.
- A sheet of paper labeled one to however many mystery boxes exist (enough for each group to have one sheet so that they may record their group's guesses for each box)

Objectives

To have students learn the body parts and the verbs associated with the five senses as well as review any previous vocabulary.

Instructions

Split the class into groups of four or five students depending on the size of the class. Give each group a "mystery box" with a mystery item inside. Once each group has a box, call out a body part associated with the five senses: eyes to see, hands or fingers to touch, ears to hear, nose to smell or mouth to taste. The students must then point to the body part and say the verb associated with it in order to identify the object: to see, to touch, to hear, to smell or to taste. Next, have the students take turns within their groups guessing what is inside their "mystery box" using only that body part you have called out to guess with. It is best to use items associated with vocabulary the students are familiar with. Cut fruit is an excellent item to use because it can be easily identified by touch, taste, and smell. Once every member within a group agrees on the item in its box, they must write that guess on the sheet of paper numbered one to whatever number of "mystery boxes" exist next to the box's corresponding number. The activity rotates until each group has guessed the items inside every box. Then the groups compare answers and the items in each box are "revealed" one by one.

Examples

In our Spanish class we used fruit so the students could smell with one box, maracas so they could shake the box and hear what sound the maracas made for another and *pan dulce* so the students could taste the sweet bread in the last box.

Pin the Part on the Body

Topic

♦ Body parts

Materials

♦ Paper body part cutouts (enough to complete an entire body)

♦ Paper bag

♦ Tape

♦ Blindfold

Objectives

To reinforce body part vocabulary

Instructions

Tape the torso of the body to the front board. Hide all other body parts in the paper bag. Create groups of four to six students, or divide the students into groups based on the classroom seating arrangement. Approach a group and ask the students, "What body part is this?" Then pull a body part cutout from the paper bag. The first student to yell out the correct name of the body part receives the body part. That student proceeds to the front of the class and is blindfolded. A piece of tape is placed on the end of the body part and the blindfolded student must then *pin* the body part on the torso. Repeat with each group until all the body parts are pinned on the board.

Examples

Our body part lesson was on Day of the Dead, so we used a cardboard skeleton for this activity rather than a normal body.

Notes

The following is a variation on this activity: Choose a student to be blindfolded. After the blindfold is put on, give the student a random body part cutout. The rest of the class shouts out the body part in unison. Now knowing the body part in hand, the blindfolded student attempts to pin the body part in the correct place. Also, to make the activity more culturally interesting, dress the body in traditional clothing of the target culture.

Skeleton Art

Topic

♦ Body parts

Materials

♦ Fill-in-the-blank skeleton worksheets

Objective

To learn the names of basic body parts

Instructions

If there is a life-size skeleton in the classroom, use it to demonstrate the body part vocabulary. Otherwise, point to students' arms, hands, feet, and so on and instruct the class to shout out the body part. After that, pass out the paper skeletons for the students to label, decorate, and cut out to hang up in the classroom.

Note

Our Spanish class used skeletons to continue our *Día de los Muertos* theme, but you may want to use animals, people, or monsters instead. We also let students choose between male and female skeletons, which they appreciated.

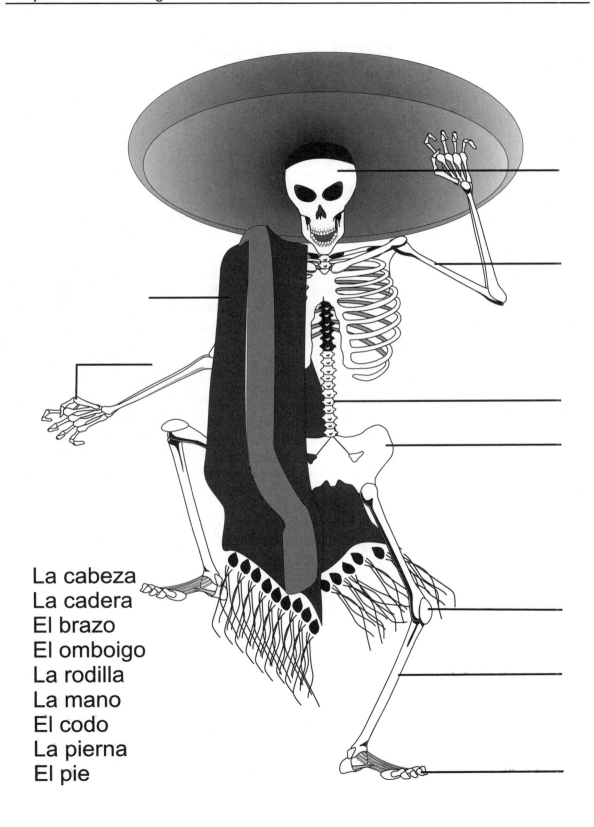

La cabeza
La cadera
El brazo
El omboigo
La rodilla
La mano
El codo
La pierna
El pie

Total Body Ball

Topic

♦ Body parts

Materials

♦ 2 to 3 medium-sized rubber playground balls

Objectives

To learn body part vocabulary and apply it to themselves

Instructions

Tell the students to sit in a circle in groups of 10 to 15, depending on the size of the class. Have the students pass a rubber ball around the circle using first their hands, then their elbows, then their feet as instructed. Once the children get used to the game, start calling out a different body part or combination of body parts each time the ball is about to be transferred from one student to the next. The student about to receive the ball must then do so using only the body part or combination of parts called out. For example, if a student received the ball using elbows, and the teacher calls out *feet* as the next body part, the student must transfer the ball still using elbows to the next student who can only use feet to receive it. If the next body parts called are *chin and chest*, the student holding the ball between his or her feet must transfer the ball still using the feet to the next person who can only receive it using neck and chin, and so on. Students may take turns sitting in the middle of the circle and directing the game once they have mastered the vocabulary.

3
Colors
and Numbers

5	3			7				
6			1	9	5			
	9	8					6	
8				6				3
4			8		3			1
7				2				6
	6					2	8	
			4	1	9			5
				8			7	9

Class Stats

Topic

- ◆ Review of numbers
- ◆ Countable vocabulary

Materials

- ◆ Colored markers
- ◆ A blank bar graph with the axes labeled (*y*-axis with numbers, *x*-axis with words or drawings of the vocabulary) for the data under investigation

Objectives

To practice vocabulary and learn how to discuss data using numbers, while directly relating numbers to the students' lives

Instructions

Choose a question that elicits quantifiable data from the students, for example, "What month is your birthday?" or "What kind of pet do you have?" Tape the bar graph to the white board and begin gathering data on the students. If time permits, ask each student the question individually to give each student a minute in the spotlight. Otherwise, pose a question about each option ("Who was born in January?" or "Who has a dog?") to the whole class and take a count of raised hands. Color in the bar graph with their responses until it is complete. Then pose a variety of questions about the data, such as "How many people have cats?" or "How many people were born in September?" The completed graph can hang in the classroom as a show of what the students accomplished.

Example

Our Japanese class made a graph about pets, including dogs, cats, birds, fish, frogs, hamsters, snakes, rabbits, and turtles. Each animal represented a bar in the graph. Because of time constraints, we asked the whole class about each animal and got a show of hands.

20

15

10

5

Art Color Match

Topic

♦ Colors

Materials

♦ Color copies of traditional or popular paintings from the target culture (1 per group)

Objectives

To reinforce knowledge of color vocabulary while experiencing art from the target culture

Instructions

To prepare for this activity, find traditional or popular paintings from the target culture and make 8.5 × 11–inch color copies of them, or print them from the Internet with a color printer. If resources are not available to make color copies for each student in the class, make enough color copies so it is feasible for the students to work in a group on this worksheet activity (no more than six students in a group). Title the worksheet *What is the color?* Draw arrows to specific colors within the painting, and connect each arrow to a *blank* where the students can label the color indicated by the arrow (see charts). After explaining the cultural significance of the paintings and/or artists, pass out the worksheets to the individual students or teams. In a team situation, students should work together and take turns writing answers.

Note

Another method is to write numbers on specific colors within the painting. In this format, students can work independently using their paper to write down the color indicated by each number.

Number Stand Off

Topic

♦ Numbers

Materials

♦ 2 sets of large cards numbered from 1 to 10

Objective

To become familiar with numbers

Instructions

Split the class into two teams. Ten students from each team come to the front and sit side by side in two lines. Give each student from both teams a card with a numbered card, in order, so that there are two lines of ten students numbered 1 to 10 sitting on the floor. The other members of the team are the callers, and they stand further back in the classroom. Face the callers with your back to the lines in front. One caller from each team comes up at a time. Hold up a sheet with a number 1 through 10 on it so that the callers can see it, but the two lines cannot. The callers call out that number to their teams in the target language, and the student with that number stands up. For example, if the number the teacher holds up is 6, the callers race to call out to their team members, "Six!" The student holding 6 must stand up. The first team with the correct student standing wins a point for their team. The team with the most points in the end wins.

Note

If team A's caller is slower than team B's, team A's line can respond to team B's command. If this becomes a problem, give a point to the first team to call out the right number and another point for the team whose *number* stands up fastest.

If you do not have a large class, you could do five numbers at a time, for example 1 to 5 or 11 to 15 and so on.

Color by Number

Topic

- ◆ Commands
- ◆ Colors
- ◆ Numbers

Materials

- ◆ Color-by-number sheet
- ◆ Crayons

Objective

To apply knowledge of colors and numbers

Instructions

On a 8.5 × 11–inch piece of paper create the color-by-number sheet. You can do so by drawing out a picture, word, or phrase and sectioning it off with lines into different-sized sections. Fill in the rest of the paper with similar randomly sized sections until the entire page is filled in and the mystery picture, word, or phrase is unrecognizable. Then, number the blank sections that to be colored in using coordinating colors and numbers, doing so for each different color needed to create the picture. The picture, word, or phrase can be recognized by contrast coloring; or if it is a drawing simply have each shape colored in to form the whole picture.

Distribute a color-by-number sheet to every student. To begin the activity, call out a number in the target language. When the students have located the section(s) containing that number, call out a color in the target language they must use to fill in that section or group of sections. Once they get comfortable with the game, call out the number and colors together to make them think on their feet to find the section and choose the correct color. The game ends when the students have filled the sheet in completely. Another way to end the game is to have students guess what the mystery picture, word, or phrase is as the sheet becomes more and more filled in. However, this usually works best on students who have learned a larger number of numbers and colors so the mystery object is harder to identify with many sections on the sheet.

Here is a color-by-number sheet of a dolphin. Note the colors that correspond to the different numbers at the bottom of the page.

1. Royal Blue	4. Orange	7. Rose
2. Light Gray	5. Yellow	8. Green
3. Blue	6. Dark Blue	9. Blue Green

Secret Codes

Topic

♦ Numbers

♦ Letters

Materials

♦ Decoding worksheet (see chart)

Objective

To learn numbers and letters

Instructions

Give students worksheets with a message coded in numbers. The key, written beneath the message, matches the numbers to their corresponding letters, such as *One = H, Two = M.* The key should contain numbers written out rather than symbols so the students learn to associate the words with the numerals.) Go over the numbers and letters with the students before they begin decoding, and again after the message is decoded.

Notes

You can add an extra step to this activity by first encoding the message in foreign numerals, such as Asian or ancient Mayan numbers, which the students must translate first to the familiar Arabic numbers and then into letters. This activity would also serve as an excellent homework assignment.

Mayan numbers worksheet:

0 ___cero___   **1** _____   **2** _____   **3** _____

   •   • •   • • •

4 _____   **5** _____   **6** ___seis___   **7** _____

• • • •   ▬▬▬   <u>•</u>▬▬   <u>• •</u>▬▬

8 _____   **9** _____   **10** _____

• • •
▬▬▬

• • • •
▬▬▬

▬▬▬
▬▬▬

▬▬▬▬▬▬▬▬▬▬▬▬▬▬
▬▬▬▬▬▬▬▬▬▬▬▬▬▬

▬▬   • • •   • •   ⬯   ▬▬   • ▬▬   • • ▬▬   • • • •
▬▬   ▬▬

Números: _____ _____ _____ _____ _____ _____ _____ _____

Letras: _____ _____ _____ _____ _____ _____ _____ _____

Números = Letras

0 = D	1 = M	2 = N	3 = P
4 = P	5 = U	6 = R	7 = A
8 = O	9 = E	10 = H	

What's The Picture?

Topic

- Numbers
- Commands

Materials

- Connect-the-dot worksheet
- Pencils, crayons, or markers

Objective

To practice numbers

Instructions

First, print or draw a picture of something simple. The picture can relate to other class activities or serve as a prelude to the next activity. Hold the picture up against a window to let the light through and trace a dotted outline of it onto a blank piece of paper. Take this sheet, randomly number the dots, and connect them lightly in pencil. Add other randomly numbered dots in random places on the page to obscure the final picture. Write down the commands you to give the students in class, such as "Draw a line from 1 to 8, from 9 to 13…." Erase any lines you made.

In class, give each student a copy of the dot-to-dot page and have them follow the instructions as you read them aloud. You can reward the first student to correctly guess the name of the object created through the dot-to-dot.

Notes

Before giving out the worksheets, make sure the students know that they are to wait for your instructions to begin. For a middle school adaptation or application, use this activity to practice the numbers 60 to 99.

4
Commands and Directions

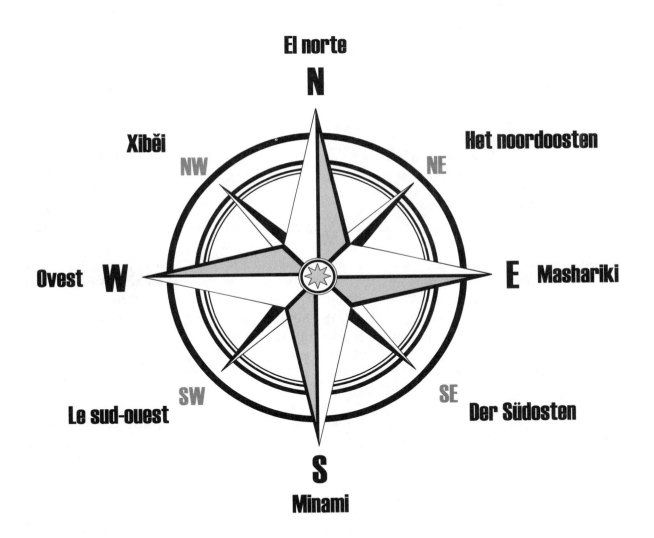

37

Dance It Up

Topic

- Directions
- Numbers
- Dance
- Music

Materials

- Stereo
- A compact disk with a popular dance song from the target culture
- A choreographed dance

Objectives

To practice directions such as *left, right, forward,* and *backward* while learning to dance a song from the target culture

Instructions

Before the lesson, choreograph a simple dance using music from the target culture. Line up the students in two rows facing the front. Turn your body to face the same way they are facing (with your back to them). Show the students the steps and have them follow and verbalize the movements with you. Add small chunks to the dance, while the students follow and repeat. After they have learned the steps, play the song and repeat the movements. While the song is playing, tell the students to say the direction they are going and the number of steps they are taking in that direction. For example, if the group is taking three steps to the right, the students can say, "To the right, one, two, three."

Example

In our Spanish class, we used the Spanish version of the song "Achy Breaky Heart" (*No Rompas Más Mi Pobre Corazón*) and we used the movements for the Electric Slide.

Notes

If it is a partner dance, you can teach the boy's and girl's parts and have them practice with partners. You can hold a dance competition by giving the partners numbers and judging a winner. For the competition, you could have the students dress in typical costume as well. If you choose to use a traditional dance, make sure that you give the students some background, such as where and how the dance originated.

Hot and Cold

Topic

- ♦ Weather
- ♦ Clothing
- ♦ Directions

Materials

- ♦ An object to hide

Objectives

To review weather or clothing vocabulary and to practice giving directions

Instructions

Send one student outside while you hide an object in the classroom. On reentering the room, classmates will direct the student to the object with hints using weather vocabulary. If he or she moves away from the object, the class calls out, "It's cold!" If the student moves closer the class yells, "It's hot!" or "It's very hot!" depending on how close the object is. And if he or she wanders far away, the class cries, "It's snowing!"

Notes

You can play a variation of this game to practice other kinds of vocabulary. For example, you can hide an article of clothing somewhere in the classroom. Leave the room and come back in quietly chanting the name of the hidden clothing. As you move closer, chant louder; as you walk farther away, chant the word more quietly. Encourage the students to chant along. Once they understand how the game works, send one student outside while you hide another article of clothing. When *it* student reenters, the other students begin chanting loudly throughout the clothing search. To make the game more difficult, hide more than one piece of clothing. The *it* student might come across one hidden object, but it is not necessarily the one the students are chanting.

In a pirate-themed variation of the game, choose two students to be the pirates and instruct them to wait briefly outside. Meanwhile the rest of the class will direct you in hiding the pirate treasure somewhere in the classroom. When the treasure is *buried*, call the two pirates back inside. The class will guide them toward the treasure by saying, "Here!" when they get close and shouting, "Over there!" when they are far. The pirate who finds the treasure first is the winner. To make the game more fun, you could give the pirates eye patches to wear.

Treasure Hunt

Topic

- ◆ Directions
- ◆ Numbers
- ◆ Geographical features

Materials

- ◆ Treasure map (see chart)
- ◆ A picture of each geographical landmark featured on the map

Objective

To practice geographical vocabulary and simple directional words (forward, backward, left, right) by leading each other around the classroom

Instructions

Tape up the pictures of the geographical landmarks around the classroom. Split students into groups and assign one landmark to each group. The entire class will look at the treasure map together to find the first landmark en route to the treasure, and the group in charge of that landmark will find its location in the room. The students in that group will then direct their classmates to it, taking turns giving commands like, "Take three steps to the left" and "Take four steps forward" until everyone reaches the picture. The class will consult the map to find the second landmark. The group in charge of that landmark will take a turn guiding the class, and so on, until all groups have a turn and they arrive at the treasure.

Examples

This game was part of a pirate-themed lesson for our Spanish class, so our map led to a pirate chest filled with chocolate gold coins. We played the game outside, which gave us more room and also made possible the occasional wildly inaccurate direction. Students said, "Fourteen steps forward," and we all walked right into a bush, at which point the group had to rethink its directions. However, the students were very careful in giving commands and considered what to say for a long time before saying it.

Note

You can tape up the geographical pictures in obvious places around the classroom; the point is not for the students to play "I Spy" with the pictures, but rather that they learn how to give accurate directions.

El mapa del tesoro

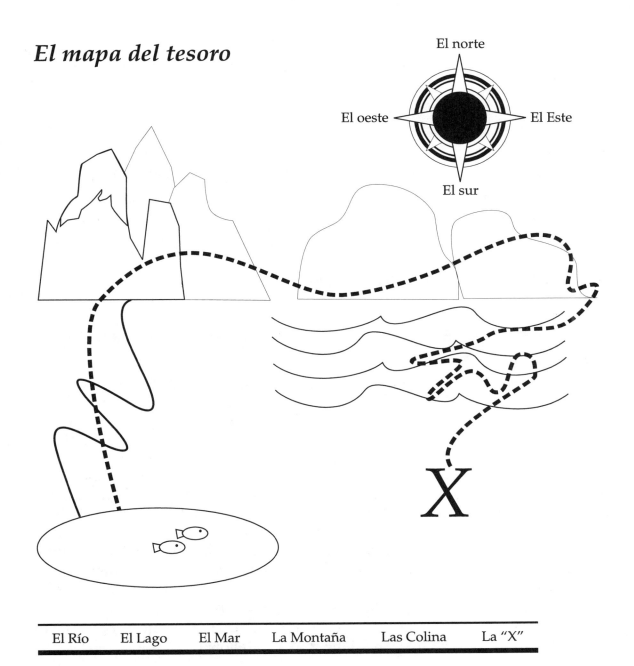

| El Río | El Lago | El Mar | La Montaña | Las Colina | La "X" |

Twister

Topic

- Directions
- Commands
- Colors
- Body parts

Materials

- 24 letter–sized, 8.5 × 11–inch sheets of paper divided into 6 of each of the following colors: yellow, red, blue and green, enough to create one twister style board
- Twister style board after the other in a straight vertical line starting from the top to bottom
- Tape to attach the colored sheets to the floor

Objectives

To practice responding to commands using body part and color vocabulary

Instructions

Split the class into two teams. On the classroom floor or outside, tape down the colored paper to create the board, or if available, use a regular twister board. Select two to three students from each team to play the first round of the game. Encourage the other group members to cheer their teammates on using encouraging phrases and exclamations from the target language during the round. To start, ask the selected students to position themselves around the outside of the board and await your first command. Then, call out a color and body part (either left or right). The selected students must place that body part on the designated color of the twister board, making sure not to move it or lift it off the board at any time. This continues until a student is unable to balance and falls, thus being eliminated from that round. The round ends when only one student is left on the board earning the team 1 point. The number of rounds the students play depends on the time allotted for the game. The team with the most points at the end of the game wins.

On the facing page is a picture of a twister style board created with color paper. In the example, R = Red; G = Green; B = Blue, and Y = Yellow.

Note

Remember to tell the students the day before to wear appropriate clothing.

R	B	Y	G
R	B	Y	G
R	B	Y	G
R	B	Y	G
R	B	Y	G
R	B	Y	G

Rough Sailing

Topic

- Directions

Materials

- None, but a large open space is preferred, and you may want to create boundaries to indicate the perimeters of the *ship*

Objective

To learn simple directions (left, right, forward, backward) in a way that gives the words a strong physical association

Instructions

Gather all the students into the middle of the ship. Let them know that seas are rough today, so they should prepare for a possible pirate attack (or shark attack, storm, or some other horrible danger). Lead them in chanting, "Row, row, row, row!" After a while, indicate that the boat has become unsteady. Shout out directions like, "Everyone to the right! Everyone to the front!" Every once in a while call out, "Pirate attack!"—or an idiomatic equivalent of "Duck and cover!"—at which point the students quickly crouch down and cover their heads. Continue to call out instructions more and more quickly. You can add an element of competition by taking students out of the game if they move too slowly or in the wrong direction. These students can join you in calling out directions.

Notes

If you play the noncompetitive version of the game, students are likely to lose interest more quickly. If you dress up as a pirate, however, students are even more engaged. This activity is also good as a traveling game, because you can pretend to sail with the students to a target country.

5
Culture

Dancing Chair

Topic

- Regional dances
- Music
- Countries or regions

Materials

- 5–10 chairs (enough for each group)
- Stereo
- Compact disk with a mix of regional songs from the target culture

Objective

To become familiar with the names and the movements of different regional dances from the target culture

Instructions

After introducing regional dances to the class, separate them into small groups of three to five students. Tell them to stand in a circle with their groups. Put a chair in the middle of the circle. Play a song from the regional dances CD, while the students dance around in their circle. When the music stops, the students must try to sit on the chair and say the name of the regional dance. The student who manages to sit and say the correct name wins that round. Then all the students who won the first round are separated into three new groups to compete in a new round. The winners from those three groups then compete in another round, until there is one winner. The regional dances between each round should change.

Example

In our Spanish class, we played music from Latin American countries. Some of the music we used was Guatemalan marimba music, Mexican *quebradita*, Argentine tango, and Cuban mambo.

Note

To make it more challenging, the students can name the type of music and its country of origin.

Mayan Ball

Topic

- ◆ Maya culture
- ◆ Body parts

Materials

- ◆ 2 hula hoops
- ◆ Beach ball
- ◆ Pictures to depict some of the more difficult words in the story such as *gods* and *twins*

Objectives

To review body part vocabulary and to learn about Maya history, specifically about the *Popol Vuh,* one of the most significant Maya texts

Instructions

There is a story in the *Popol Vuh* about the creation of the Mayan ball game. The first part of the story describes the unlucky fate of two twins who play ball and lose against the gods of death. Tell this story to the class twice to ensure that the students understand it. Use lots of total physical response (TPR), encouraging the students to join in calling out words and making the motions at different points in the story. Afterward, go outside and split the students into two teams, *twins* and *gods.* One person from each team stands on either side of the rectangular court and holds the hula hoops. The rules of the game are simple: Only elbows, knees, and hips may be used to touch the ball; and the first team to put the ball through their hoop wins.

Example

We told this simplified, abridged version of the history of the Mayan ball game. The italic words had specific TPR actions associated with them:

Hay dos gemelos— hermanos idénticos. Se llaman Hun-Hunahpu y Vucub Hunahpu.

Son buenísimos jugadores con la *pelota* (mimic bouncing a ball).

Juegan con la pelota todos los días.

Están muy *ruidosos* (yell this word) y los Dioses los oyen.

Los Dioses se hacen *enojados* (make an angry face).

Los Dioses enojados quieren *desterrar* (point forcefully toward the door) a Hun-Hunahpu y Vucub Hunahpu.

Dicen a los gemelos: "¡Oyen! Queremos tener una competición.

Jugamos (pass the ball back and forth) con la *pelota.*

Si nosotros *ganamos* (arms up in the air in a *victory* pose), los *desterramos*.

Si ustedes *ganan,* no los *desterramos.*

Ellos empiezan a *jugar* con la *pelota.* Juegan por muchos días.

Los Dioses *enojados hacen trampas* (pretend to pass the ball to the students. When they reach out to take it, snatch it away and laugh) y *ganan* la competición.

Destierran a los gemelos.

Ahora están *felices* (big smile) porque nadie *juega* con la *pelota.*

Y nadie es *ruidoso.*

Note

You could most likely adapt this game for a class that teaches another language, because folktales and sports are an important part of all cultures.

I Fold

Topic

- Origami
- Culture

Materials

- Origami paper (2 squares per student)
- Scrap paper (2 squares per student)

Objectives

To participate in cultural activities such as origami, as well as to learn the vocabulary associated with that activity

Instructions

Give each student two squares of plain paper for practice sheets and two pieces of nice origami paper. The students use a sheet of practice paper to follow along with you as you demonstrate the first design (perhaps a crane for origami). Once they have completed a design with the practice paper, go through the steps again using the nice paper. If there is time, repeat with a different design.

Example

Our Japanese class made a simple origami box. We had plans to make a crane as well, but we had limited time.

Note

Allow a lot of time for this activity, because origami can be complicated, especially for children. However, the students are sure to have a good time, and they have a neat thing to take home with them.

Khipu Count

Topic

♦ Family

♦ Numbers

♦ Incan knot system

Materials

♦ String (or yarn) 1foot long (enough for each student)

♦ String (or yarn) at least 1 yard long

Objectives

To practice using the names of family members while learning the Incan khipu system and reviewing their numbers

Instructions

The khipu is a knot system that was used by the ancient Incan civilization. Its uses remain unknown; but some anthropologists theorize that it was used as a census count, a writing system, or for basic mathematical uses. In this activity, students create their own khipu to use as a census count for their immediate family and their classmates. Introduce the history of the Incan khipu to the students. Provide each student with a long piece of string, and demonstrate the process of making a knot. A khipu knot is made like any other knot. The students should repeat and follow the steps to make a knot. Tell them to make one for each family member. Each knot should look different depending on the family member it represents. For instance, the *mother* and *father* knots are bigger than the *brother knot. When the class is finished, ask for volunteers to present each knot by saying which family member it represents. Then tell them to count the number of family member knots on their stings. After presenting, they should tie their family khipu to the class khipu. The class khipu is made by using an extra long piece of string and having students tie their string to it. At the end, the class counts all the knots in the class khipu to determine the census for their class and family.*

Who's the Star?

Topic

- ◆ Celebrities
- ◆ Occupations
- ◆ Target culture

Materials

- ◆ Pictures of several celebrities from the target country and their American counterparts

Objectives

To become familiar with the terms for different kinds of celebrities (sports player, singer, president, actor, band, etc.) and key celebrity figures from the target country

Instructions

After teaching the students the words for various kinds of celebrities from the target country, test their memory with this game. Split the class into as many teams as you have types of celebrities (five to six is ideal). Starting with the first team, show them a picture first of an American celebrity. Ask the team to name that celebrity and say what kind celebrity he or she is. The team gets a point for the name and another point for the occupation of the celebrity. If the team cannot come up with the answer, the play is opened to the class. Each team gets a chance to name the American celebrities. In the second round, the students are shown pictures of celebrities from the target country, and they must remember their names and occupations. The team with the most points in the end wins.

Note

If you mention they will be asked to remember the names of the celebrities with a game when teaching the names, the students will make a much greater effort to remember them.

6

Date and Time

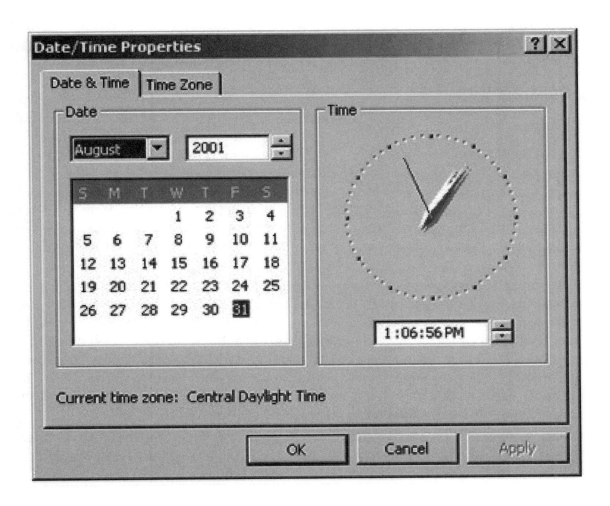

Cultural Memory Clock

Topic

♦ Telling time and culture

Materials

♦ 2 large cardboard clocks

Objectives

To practice telling time through examining different cultural activities at different times of the day, afternoon, evening, and night

Instructions

The clocks should be at least twice the size of a standard schoolroom clock with moveable hands to tell the time (moveable hands are created by fastening the clock hands to the cardboard clock with a brad). One clock represents the early morning and day (1 a.m.–12 p.m.) and the other the afternoon and night (1 p.m.–12 a.m.). To add a cultural element to the clocks, select at least four times of day on each clock. Then next to the selected times, draw pictures of an activity a student from the target culture might be engaged in during that time of the day or night. Lastly, cover the drawing with a Post-it note or piece of paper so that it can be removed and replaced easily.

The activity operates like a story, with the clock acting as the book. Turn the hands of the clock to a time with a picture drawn next to it. Remove the Post-it or piece of paper and tell the students, "At _____ o'clock, [name of student from target culture] [does certain activity]." Have the class repeat the sentence at least twice, then ask the class what the student from the target language does at that time to have them practice the sentence once more in a question-and-answer format to prepare them for the activity. Go through each picture on the clocks in this same way once, covering up the activities once the class has practiced the sentence a few times.

Next, divide the class into two teams. Alternating between the two teams, choose one student to come up to the clock and move its hands to a time of day or night depending on which clock they have chosen. The student chooses a time and says, "It is _____ o'clock." If he or she states the time correctly, the team gets a point. If a time of day or night that corresponds to an activity is chosen, the student must first state the time correctly and if correct has a chance to guess which activity the target student does during that time. The team wins 2 points for every correct answer, and the activity is uncovered so it cannot be guessed again during that round. The game goes on until all the activities are uncovered. The team with the most points wins.

Example

In my Spanish class we had a young student, Manuela, make tortillas for breakfast at 6 in the morning, go to school at 8, come home for lunch at 11 and go to the park at 12. For the evening clock, Manuela did her homework at 3, went to salsa dance class at 5, helped her mother cook dinner at 6, and went to bed at 9.

Note

The activity can be made more difficult by increasing the number of activities drawn on the clock.

Fly to Find the Criminal

Topic

♦ Time

Materials

♦ A schedule of flight times from a local airport to various cities or countries that speak the target language; flight times can be written as numbers or as words (1:00 or one o'clock)

♦ A representation of the stolen object perhaps made out of butcher paper

Objectives

To practice telling time in the target language

Instructions

Decide if you will act as the criminal or if you will ask a student before the game starts. Instruct the *criminal* to walk sneakily around the classroom and wait to be *caught* by the students when they arrive at a certain city or country. To begin the game, tell the students that something has been stolen from the target culture. Pass out the flight schedules and ask the students where they want to fly first to search for the criminal. Tell them the current time and see if they can find a flight that is taking off shortly. Call on students to tell you which flight they want (where to and at what time). After the class pretends to fly to that location (arms out and with airplane noises), have the students look around the classroom for the criminal, either standing up, or remaining seated. If they do not find the criminal, they fly back home. There, let another student decide where to fly to see if the criminal is in that city or country. When the students arrive at the predetermined location of the criminal, the criminal pretends to hide the stolen object and tiptoe around the classroom. Act surprised and tell the students to capture the criminal by surrounding her or tapping her lightly.

Example

The stolen object can be a monument like the Eiffel Tower or Machu Picchu, the class mascot, and so forth.

Notes

The criminal can be caught either in the country of origin, or in another city and country. Also, you do not have to pass out a flight schedule. Instead, you can let the students shout out where they want to fly and then look at a pretend schedule to tell them what time the plane leaves. Or, you can write the departure time on the board and have the students call out that time. This activity can involve as little or as much practice with time telling as you like.

Schedule Yourself

Topic

- Days of the week

- Activities

Materials

- A schedule for each student: a piece of paper divided into seven columns, one for each day of the week

- An enlarged version of the blank schedule for demonstration of the activity

- Many small labeled pictures of different activities the students do

- Large versions of these pictures for the demonstration

Objectives

To learn the days of the week and practice the names of different activities

Instructions

Label each column of your sample schedule with a day of the week. Next, demonstrate with the sample schedule that the students will be taping or gluing the different activity cards to the day of the week in which they do those activities. Ask them, for example, "What day do I go to school?" or "What day should I cook dinner?" Next, pass out the cards and the blank schedules to the students and have them create their own schedules. For less preparation, the students could draw their own pictures and label them with the appropriate descriptions.

Examples

Activities could include going to school (ensure you have enough for each student to show that students go to school five times a week), playing sports, talking with friends, cooking dinner, babysitting a younger sibling, playing an instrument, going to church/temple/mosque, and so on.

Full Schedule

Topic

- ◆ Dates
- ◆ Days of the week
- ◆ Activities

Materials

- ◆ Photocopies of a calendar page for each student with drawings of a different activity for every day of the week, but they do not have to be all in the same week (see example)

Objectives

To learn to connect the days of the week to dates and also to teach typical activities of children from the target country

Instructions

Split the class into several teams. Beginning with the first team, ask the students to look at their calendars and tell you what the imaginary target culture child does on a certain date that has an activity drawn on it, for example, the 8th or the 27th (whichever dates have a picture of an activity on the calendar page). Students get a point for naming the correct activity. Next ask what day of the week that is. If they get that correct, they get another point. If the students do not know the answer, play is opened to the class. Continue until all the teams get an equal number of chances. The team with the most points in the end wins.

Example

Before our Japanese class played this game, we showed a large calendar with one whole week filled in with activities. We had our imaginary Japanese child, Tarou, play violin on Mondays, play baseball on Tuesdays, practice video games on Wednesday, attend judo on Thursdays, sing karaoke on Fridays, see a movie on Saturdays, and do his homework on Sundays. Then on the calendar page, we kept the activities on the same days of the week, but spread them out over various weeks, so that on the Tuesday of one week he would play baseball, and on Thursday of the next week practice judo, and so on.

Sunday	Monday	Tuesday	Wednesday	Thursday	Friday	Saturday
	1	2	3	4	5	6
7	8	9	10	11	12	13
14	15	16	17	18	19	20
21	22	23	24	25	26	27
28	29	30				

Human Bar Graph

Topic

- ◆ Time
- ◆ Daily schedules

Materials

- ◆ A picture or another visual representation of a student from the target culture, like a doll or a stuffed animal
- ◆ A list of activities you plan to graph, such as waking up, eating breakfast, going to school, eating lunch, returning home, taking a siesta, eating dinner, and bedtime
- ◆ Time signs

Objective

To gain an appreciation of a typical day in the life of a student in the target culture

Instructions

Make time signs on brightly colored pieces of paper denoting different times of day, color-coded to correspond to the various daily activities, such as breakfast times on blue signs and lunch times on red. For each different activity, make approximately five signs on half-hour intervals. The breakfast set, for example, could include 6:30, 7:00, 7:30, 8:00, and 8:30.

Begin by recounting to the class a typical weekday in the life of a student from the target culture. Draw a clock on the whiteboard and move the hands around as the student goes through the day. After that, tell the students that they are all going to make a *human graph* to compare her schedule to ours. Place the *waking up* signs on the floor to designate the left-to-right axis of the graph. Then set the picture of the foreign student behind, for example, the 7:30 sign. Say to the class, "Émilie wakes up at 7:30. Does anyone here wake up at 7:30? At 7:00? At 6:30?" Students come up and stand behind the appropriate signs, like bars on a graph. When everyone is standing, exclaim over the results: "Émilie sleeps in much later than most of you!" Ask what they observe about the similarities and differences in their schedules. Then go on to graph breakfast time, dinnertime, bedtime, and so on as time allows.

Note

You can make the game more difficult in later rounds by asking individual students what times they go to bed or eat dinner, requiring verbal answers rather than raised hands.

6:00	6:30	7:00	7:30	8:00

◯ ◯ ◯ (Émilie)

◯ ◯ ◯

◯ ◯

◯ ◯

Interactive Story Book

Topic

♦ Days of the week and cultural activities

Materials

♦ 24 × 18–inch (or similar large size) story book

♦ Paper cut-outs corresponding to actions within the story

♦ Poster-sized chart with a different day of the week for each heading

Objectives

To learn the days of the week through association with day-to-day activities for each day

Instructions

Gather the students around you. Inform them they will be read a short story about a week in the life of a normal student their age from a country speaking the target language. The story should start on Monday because students in the United States associate the beginning of a new week with the first day of school. For Monday through Friday, the student in the story should travel to school every day in addition to doing one other activity. For example, "On Monday, Pepe goes to school and then plays soccer with his friends." Then on Saturday and Sunday the student in the story should do one or two culturally relevant activities. During the story, have students repeat the day of the week and the action completed that day after it is read for example, "Monday, school, play soccer." When the story is complete, ask students to volunteer to place cutouts representing the actions completed (e.g., a picture of a school or a soccer ball) on a large chart under the correct day the action was completed in the story. Make sure to ask the class to confirm whether or not the cutout was placed on the correct day.

On the following page there is a sample chart from my Spanish class using Pepe as our target student:

Example

In our Spanish class, we had Pepe go to school Monday through Friday, play soccer on Tuesdays and Thursdays after school, and do his homework on Wednesdays and Fridays. On Saturday, he attended a *fiesta* for a friend's birthday, and on Sunday he went to church with his family.

Lunes	Martes	Miercoles	Jueves	Viernes	Sábado	Domingo

Time Out

Topic

- ◆ Time
- ◆ Numbers

Materials

- ◆ 4 signs or mats designating different times of day, such as 3:00, 8:00, or something more difficult like 8:47
- ◆ Small pieces of paper denoting times that correspond to those on the signs or mats
- ◆ Music from the target culture (for a lively atmosphere)

Objectives

To review numbers and practice telling time

Instructions

If you play inside, place the signs on four tables around the classroom. If you go outside, set up mats on the ground. Give the students 10 seconds to disperse randomly to one of the tables or mats. Count down the seconds loudly. When you finish counting, the students at each table or mat will yell out the time written there. Then choose a student to blindly draw one of the small pieces of paper out of a hat, read aloud the time written there, and return the paper to the hat. The students grouped at the corresponding table or mat are *out* and must sit down. The remaining students have 10 seconds to move to another table or remain at the same one if they choose, and then another student will draw a paper from the hat. This continues until only one student is left standing.

Examples

Because there were two teachers in our Spanish class, one of us played the game with the students while the other stayed at the front. This helped students figure out the game more quickly and prevented any blatant cheating. If you teach alone, perhaps you can have a native speaker act as game mediator.

Notes

You can also use the music to play a sort of *musical mats.* Students dance around while the music plays, and when it stops, they run to one of the mats or tables. Start the music again to indicate a new round. To keep the *out* students involved in the game, you can have them continue to yell out the times with the rest of the students and count down the seconds between rounds with you. You can play this game with other vocabulary as well, such as animals, weather, or food.

Travel Itinerary

Topic

♦ Dates

♦ Time

Materials

♦ Floor map

♦ Itinerary note cards

♦ Photographs or drawings of points of interest in each city

Objectives

To incorporate students' knowledge of dates and times with a travel simulation that teaches students about the cities in a target country

Instructions:

For the floor map, on a large piece of butcher paper, draw a map of a country that speaks the target language. Choose several cities in the country that are culturally or geographically significant, and label them on the map.

To make the itinerary note cards, write out an *itinerary* on each note card. For example, on one note card write, "September 17th," and write a city name below the date. On another note card write, "September 18th," and a different city name below this date. If you have seven cities, write out seven itinerary note cards.

Place the map on the floor so it is visible to all students. Next, ask for volunteers to be *travelers*. Each volunteer will receive an itinerary. Announce, "Today is September 17th. Where are we going today?" The student with the itinerary note card for September 17th will walk onto the map and stand on the correct city. At this point, briefly explain the significance of that city, showing photographs or drawings when necessary. Continue with the other itineraries in this manner, allowing each volunteer to stand on the city indicated on her itinerary note card.

Note

This activity could also incorporate time in the itinerary. For example, the itinerary could be "3:30 p.m. September 17th" instead of simply "September 17th."

7

Family and the Home

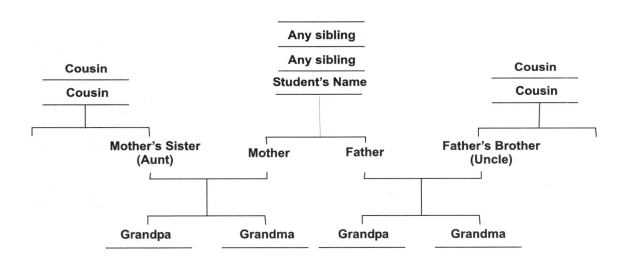

Family Tree Interview

Topic

- Family vocabulary
- Questions of quantity
- Names

Materials

- 1 blank sheet of white paper for each student
- Writing utensils

Objectives

To have students apply family vocabulary to their own families

Instructions

Divide students into pairs, giving each student a piece of white paper. Students then *interview* their partners, basing family trees on the interviews. Have each student write the partner's name at the top of the page and ask how many brothers or sisters he or she has. For replies other than zero, the student draws that many lines next to the partner's name. The student then asks the partner for sibling names and fills them in the blank lines. This process is repeated for parents and grandparents using lines to distinguish between generations. For a more complicated activity, partners can ask each other about extended family such as uncles, aunts, or cousins. The activity is completed when each partner has created a family tree based on the interview. The family trees may be shared as a class or in groups depending on the amount of time allotted for the activity.

A template for a student's family tree is on the preceding page.

The Lively Family Tree

Topic

♦ Family

Materials

♦ Costumes to portray each family member

♦ Family tree chart

♦ Family member cards

Objective

To practice family vocabulary

Instructions

Draw a simple family tree on butcher paper, leaving blank spaces for all the members that will be taught. It may be helpful to put a pink or blue circle around each blank space to indicate if the family member is male or female.

Create the family member cards (to place in each of the blank spaces of the chart) by either drawing a picture of the specific family member or writing out the word for the specific family member. It is necessary to establish one child to base the family on. For example, give a proper name to one of the children, so we can understand the family members as that child's *grandmother, father, brother,* and so on.

Hang the family tree chart in the front of the classroom. Then, you, an aide, or a volunteer leaves the room to dress up as a specific family member. When the *family member* enters the classroom, the first student to correctly guess what family member depicted receives the corresponding family member card. The student then places the family member card in the correct blank space on the family tree chart.

Example

You enter the classroom dressed in a cap, carrying a cane, and walking hunched over. You say, "Hello," in a shaky, old voice. A student correctly guesses that you are depicting the grandfather. This student then receives the grandfather family member card and proceeds to the front of the classroom to put the card at the top of the family tree chart in the blue circle blank space.

Note

It may be difficult to act out aunt, uncle, and cousin; but you could teach these by placing their family member cards on the chart after the grandparents, parents, and children are already placed on the chart.

House Hunt

Topic

- ◆ Rooms
- ◆ Household items
- ◆ Verb *to be (located)*

Materials

- ◆ Question mark paper cutout, a large question mark cut from bright-colored construction paper
- ◆ Large drawing of a house (see chart), clearly showing the different types of rooms (bedroom, living room, bathroom, etc); each room incorporating common household items found in your classroom (sink, window, door, computer, floor, etc.)

Objectives

To practice household items vocabulary and learn to identify the rooms where the items are located

Instructions

Divide the class into numbered groups. Tell the students to put their heads down on their desks (no peeking!) while you place the question mark on one of the vocabulary items in the classroom (sink, window, door, computer, floor, etc.) After doing so, yell out a group number. At this point, students can lift their heads, but only the specified group can stand up and begin to *hunt* for the special item. The first student to find the special item must touch the question mark and yells out the correct vocabulary word. This student *wins* and is then asked to identify in which room the item is located. For example, if the question mark item was on the sink, ask the winning student, "Where is the sink?" while holding up the drawing of the house. The student responds, "The sink is in the bathroom." The game proceeds in this fashion.

Old Maid

Topic

- ◆ Family
- ◆ Verb *to have*
- ◆ Review
- ◆ Numbers

Materials

- ◆ 4 to 6 decks of fifty 3 × 5–inch note cards
- ◆ Colored pencils, pens, or crayons (enough for every student to use some)
- ◆ Old Maid cards (enough that every group of students has one 3 × 5–inch Old Maid note card in their deck, making the final number of cards in each deck 51)

Objectives

To practice family vocabulary and the verb *to have* through interaction with fellow classmates

Instructions

To create the Old Maid card, simply draw a picture of an unpleasant-looking old woman with the words *Old Maid* written underneath the drawing.

Divide students into groups of four to six depending on the size of the class. Hand out a blank *deck* of cards to each group. On one side of the note cards, instruct students to draw pictures of different family members making sure that their deck of cards has an even number of each kind of family member in it. Within their group, students can decide which family members they wish to draw, as long as nobody draws a picture of the Old Maid. Typical family members to draw on the cards are father, mother, sister, brother, grandma, grandpa, uncle, aunt, cousin (female), cousin (male), stepbrother or stepsister, half brother or sister and so on. Below the drawing of the family member, students must write the general name (mother, father, sister, etc.) of that person to avoid any confusion among similar-looking family members such as male cousin and brother.

Once all the cards have been drawn, pass out an Old Maid card to each group to shuffle into their decks. After the cards are shuffled, they are dealt out one by one within the group until none are left (someone ends up with an extra card because there are an odd number but this does not matter). Next, students take turns randomly selecting a card from the person sitting to her right, adding it to her own hand. In this way, every member of the group has the same probability of ending up with the Old Maid card. Whenever a pair of two family members in, the student must show the group the pair and say, for example, "I have two mothers" or "I have two Grandpas" and place the pair on the table. The game ends when all of the pairs have been matched leaving one student with the Old Maid card.

Notes

Once all of the cards are created, this game can be played over and over whenever students have time or wish to play. This game could be used with a variety of vocabulary as long as one card is kept as the Old Maid to distinguish it from the others. In addition, to save time during class, creating the playing cards could be assigned as homework the previous night. Remember that when playing the game during class, it is better to keep the groups as small as possible because that gives each student a greater opportunity to speak when pairing their cards and showing them to the group.

Run to Mother

Topic

♦ Family trees

Materials

♦ A large family tree laid out on the ground with a large sheet of paper representing each family member

Objectives

To learn how family members are related

Instructions

To make the family tree, draw pictures of different family members on large sheets of paper and lay them out in the shape of a family tree with string or strips of paper showing the bonds and relations.

Before class, lay out a large family tree outside on the ground. Take the class outside, split them into four teams, and line up each team equidistantly around the family tree. Call out the name of a family member (i.e., "sister," or "father"). The first student in each line runs and taps the correct person in the family tree. Whoever taps the family member first wins a point for the team. Continue through each student in the lines. The team with the most points in the end wins. If the students are catching on too quickly, make the game more complicated by saying, for example, "Father's sister," so the students tap *aunt*.

Note

Be sure to have a clear *me* in the family tree, or else *mother* could be a relative term, such as aunt (mother of cousins) or grandmother (mother of mother).

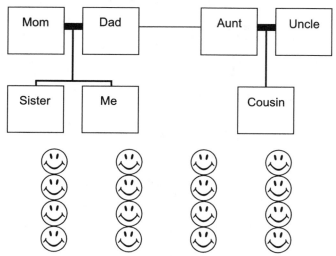

8
Food

Bake Time

Topic

- Ingredients
- Cooking terms

Materials

- A recipe for a baked good (e.g., bread or cake)
- All the ingredients necessary to make the food. Have a small, labeled bowl or container for each ingredient. The bowls 'need not be filled with the actual ingredients because the students do not eat what they are *baking*. A similar-looking ingredient is fine. For example, salt can also be used for sugar and baking soda. For eggs, plastic Easter eggs can be used, students can pretend to crack them open and add them into the mixing bowl.
- Mixing bowl
- Spoon for mixing
- *Oven* (such as an empty garbage can turned on its side and labeled *Oven*)
- Actual baked good to give to the students after the mixture has *cooked* in the oven

Objectives

To sample a traditional baked good and learn the vocabulary associated with cooking

Instructions

Lay out the ingredients in little bowls on a table at the front of the room. Call on students join you in the front of the classroom and instruct them to add an ingredient to the mixing bowl; for example, "Add the salt." They must look at the names on the small bowls to find the right ingredient and add it. Have other students come up to add other ingredients. One student mixes all the ingredients together at the end. Put the *dough* (note: may not be edible) in the "oven" until it's all done. Take the prebaked goods out of the *oven* and give samples to all the students. It would be great if the baked goods can fit in the oven and still have room to put the *dough* bowl in the oven. That way, the baked goods can hide in the oven until the *dough* magically bakes and you can surprise the students by pulling out the finished product.

Examples

Conchas is Mexican bread and baguettes are typical bread from France.

Notes

If you bring in the real ingredients and have access to an oven, it is a great idea to actually cook the baked good.

Baker's Puzzle

Topic

- Baking

Materials

- Written list of bread ingredients, displayed in a prominent place (whiteboard, overhead, etc.)
- Pictures of the ingredients
- Butcher paper puzzle: a loaf of bread drawn on butcher paper and cut up into pieces; number of pieces matches the number of ingredients
- Puzzle frame: an outline of the completed puzzle on plain butcher paper to assist students in placing the pieces
- Bowl
- Spoon
- Loaf of bread for the students to eat afterward

Objectives

To learn about a food popular in the target culture and the vocabulary associated with it

Instructions

Prepare by putting the puzzle pieces into the mixing bowl. Then call on student volunteers to name the bread ingredients, giving them the corresponding pictures to hold onto until later. When all the pictures are distributed, point to the list and ask the class, "What is the first ingredient we add?" Everyone yells out the answer. The student holding the picture of that ingredient comes up, drops the picture in the bowl, and mixes it up with the spoon while you and the class chant, "Mix, mix, mix!" Removing a puzzle piece from the bowl, the student tapes it onto the picture frame. Continue with the next ingredients on the list, asking different students to *add and mix*. By the end of the game, all the pictures of the ingredients are in the bowl and all the puzzle pieces are out of it. When the puzzle is completed, bring out the loaf of bread to share with the class.

Example

This game was part of our Spanish class's celebration of *Día de los Muertos*. Although most students did not get a turn with the puzzle (we had nine ingredients and therefore nine puzzle pieces), everyone got caught up in the game, shouting "Mix, mix!" and cheering when a classmate fit a piece correctly.

Note

You can also play this game to review body part vocabulary by instructing students to mix with their elbows, knees, left and right hands, and heads, instead of with the spoon. Students can join in calling out the body parts they want their classmates to use.

Chef's Choice

Topic

- ◆ Food
- ◆ Cooking
- ◆ Ingredients

Materials

- ◆ Play dough
- ◆ Real example of the food being made (enough for the whole class to eat)
- ◆ Newspaper
- ◆ 1 chef's hat
- ◆ Sets of empty jars (any size) labeled with pictures of ingredients; 1 jar for each ingredient and a set of jars for each group

Objectives

To use food vocabulary and verbs involved with cooking, while learning the steps needed to make traditional food from the target culture

Instructions

Homemade play dough is made by mixing 2 cups of flour, 1 cup of salt, and 1/4 cup of oil. Then add 3/4 cup of water and knead until soft.

Separate the class into small groups of three to five students. Give each group a set of jars and each member some play dough. Put on the chef's hat and tell the students, "Today, we are cooking [insert food name]." Show the students a finished example of the food you are cooking. Using play dough, go through the steps involved in making the food. The empty jars can be used to add pretend ingredients. The students should repeat the actions and the names of ingredients. When the class has finished making the food out of play dough, ask them questions about the process involved in making the food. For example, you can lift a jar and ask for the name of the ingredient. The first student to correctly answer the question receives a piece of the real food item for her team. Continue asking questions until all the groups have gotten food.

Notes

Here are foods than can be made according to the target language:

- ◆ French: Crêpe
- ◆ Italian: Pasta
- ◆ Spanish: Tortilla
- ◆ Japanese: Sushi

Fruit Salad

Topic

♦ Fruit

Materials

♦ 5 types of fruits, cut into bite-seized pieces, equal to the number of students minus one in each group

♦ Ziplock bags for all but one person per group to have a bag filled with cut fruit (1 bag of each fruit for each group and for yourself)

♦ A big bowl and mixing spoon for each group

♦ A toothpick for each person

Objective

To learn about the fruits popular in the target country

Instructions

After teaching the names of the fruits, pass out the bowls, bags of fruit, and spoons so that one member of each group has the mixing spoon and the others have the fruit. Before handing out the fruit, bowl, and spoon, have the students tell you the name of the object they are receiving. Make sure the students understand they are not to open the baggies until told to do so. Hold up one of your baggies and have the students identify the fruit. Next, have each student with that fruit stand up and show you her bag. Instruct these students to open their ziplock bags and empty them into the big bowl. Repeat this process for each fruit. Once all the fruit is added, have the students with the spoons mix their group's fruit salad. Finally, pass out a toothpick to each student and let the students eat the group's creation.

Notes

For a Latin flavor, you can include fruits like jicama and lime to squeeze on their salads. It is also a good idea to bring an uncut example of each fruit to show the students.

Fruit Tasting Challenge

Topic

- Fruits
- Vegetables
- Other foods

Materials

- Chopped fruits or vegetables
- Toothpicks

Objective

To learn food vocabulary

Instructions

Divide students into two lines and call the first person in each line to come forward. Blindfold them and give both an identical piece of fruit on a toothpick to taste. The first student to correctly name the fruit wins a point for her team. Then both return to the back of the lines and the next two students step forward. Continue until each student has had a turn. You can make the game a little more complicated as time goes on by giving students two fruits to taste and requiring that they correctly guess both to earn points.

Example

Our Spanish class played this game with five fruits: apples, oranges, grapes, lemons, and pomegranates. The *weird-tasting* fruits (lemon and pomegranate) were most popular, and students who had already undergone the tasting challenge had fun whispering to us which fruit to give their classmates.

The Market Special

Topic

- ◆ Fruits

- ◆ Vegetables

- ◆ Courtesy expressions (*please, thank you, you're welcome*)

- ◆ Shopping

Materials

- ◆ Paper money from the target culture

- ◆ Fruits and vegetables (real or crafted)

- ◆ Table

- ◆ Items to make the market scene more cultural (i.e., traditional Mexican blanket to spread on the table for a Mexican market)

- ◆ *The Special* cards

Objectives

To use student's knowledge of fruit and vegetable vocabulary, courtesy expressions, and shopping phrases in an interactive, traditional market experience

Instructions

Using construction paper or note cards, write *The Special* on one side of the card and leave the other side blank for the activity. Before the start of each round, secretly take three The Special cards and write a different item on the backside of each card.

Create groups of four to six students, or divide the students into groups based on the classroom seating arrangement. Give a number to each group or table. Give each group an equal amount of paper money. Call out a group or table number. A representative from that group comes up to the market and asks, "How much does the [fruit or vegetable] cost?" The merchant (either the teacher or another student) responds, "It costs ____." The buyer replies, "The [fruit or vegetable], please." The buyer pays with paper money and says, "Thank you," when the merchant gives the student buyer the item; and the merchant responds, "You're welcome." The activity proceeds in the same sequence until all groups have purchased an item. Then reveal the three "The Special" cards. Announce those items, and if any group purchased a *special item* for that round, they receive *The Special* card and earn 10 points for their group. Complete as many rounds as time and items available.

May I Take Your Order?

Topic

- Food

Materials

- Blank menus (two pieces of construction paper stapled together works well)

- Note cards or paper for the waiter/waitress to write down orders

- Aprons for the waiter and waitress, possibly made out of white butcher paper and string (optional)

Objectives

To learn food vocabulary, typical meals in the target culture, and how to make and take food orders

Instructions

Brainstorm with the students about what to write on their menus for breakfast, lunch, and dinner; and then write on the board the menu options that they should copy onto their blank menus. After the students have copied down the menu items, teach the phrases, "May I take your order?" and "I would like...." Divide the students into groups of approximately five and have the students take turns playing waiter or waitress. The waiter or waitress for the group asks members what they would like to order and writes it down. When everyone has ordered, someone else from the group becomes the waiter or waitress.

Notes

Our Spanish class took two class periods, or two 15-minute sessions, to complete this activity. The first day we made the menus, and the second day the students took each other's orders.

Pass the Potato

Topic

- Fruits and vegetables
- Any objects

Materials

- Several fruits and/or vegetables that can be easily handled (i.e., orange, apple, pear, but not pineapple)
- Traditional music of the target culture

Objectives

To reinforce and test 'knowledge of fruit and/or vegetable vocabulary along with the use of the verb *to have*

Instructions

Create groups of four to six students, or divide the students into groups based on the classroom seating arrangement. Give a fruit or vegetable to each group. The students begin passing the item around their group when the music starts. When the music stops, ask each student with the item in hand, "What fruit or vegetable do you have?" The student responds, "I have the _____." If the student answers correctly, the group receives 1 point. After each round, switch the fruits and vegetables among the groups so students have different items to identify.

Notes

Pass the Potato is easily adapted to other vocabulary if the items can be physically passed around the group.

9
Language

Pronunciation, Idiomatic Expressions, and Parts of Speech

Ee

elephant   elefante

Pronoun Hat Dance

Topic

- Personal pronouns

Materials

- Hat crowns (one for each student)

Objective

To gain an understanding of personal pronouns

Instructions

Hat crowns are constructed by first picking a hat that hails from a culture speaking the target language. Draw a picture of the hat or print one off the Internet. To make the picture into a crown, simply take a thin strip of paper and staple it together to form a circle large enough to fit on a student's head. Then attach the drawing or photo to the circular strip.

Divide students into groups of two. While they are wearing hat crowns on their heads, instruct the students to stand side by side next to their partners. To begin the game, place yourself in middle of the class and shout out one personal pronoun at a time, such as *I, you, he, she, they,* or *we.* Students must respond with a different physical movement for each command. For *I* students make a *thumbs up* motion and point to themselves using both thumbs. For *you* students point to their partners with one finger. For *he* or *she* students point with one finger to a boy or girl in another group. For *they* students point with both hands towards another group. For *we* students join hands and lift them into the air in unison. To make the game more challenging, students can integrate their hat crowns into various commands. For *I* students lift the hat crown on and off their head. For *you* have them switch hat crowns with their partner, and for *we* students wave their hats in the air in unison with their partner.

Example

In my Spanish class, our students wore sombrero hat crowns. The crowns were constructed from a yellow strip of paper stapled to form the circle, with a drawing of a sombrero stapled to the front of the crown.

Exclamation Station

Topic
- Idiomatic exclamations
- Simple phrases
- Travel vocabulary

Materials
- A list of at least 10 idiomatic exclamations and simple phrases common to the target language
- A scenario page with a description of a scene to be acted out by the students; the most successful have to do with travel, such as buying a ticket, hailing a taxi, or any daily activity involving brief exchanges

Objectives
To learn common idiomatic expressions and short phrases and apply them to everyday activities

Instructions
This activity is carried out using only exclamations and two-word phrases native to the target language. During this activity, the class can be split into any number of groups, small or large, depending on how many exclamations and scenarios you wish to provide. Once the groups are formed, give the students a list of exclamations and two-word phrases common to the target language. The students must act out their scenario speaking only in exclamations and short phrases. After each group has practiced, they must perform for the class. Their classmates must then guess what the performance depicts.

Some common Spanish expressions are as follows:

- ¡Oye!
- ¡Claro!
- ¡Caramba!
- ¡Qué Lástima!
- ¡Por Favor!
- ¡Gracias!
- ¡Vamonos!

French expressions could include the following

- Bien Sûr!
- Oui!
- D'accord!
- Merci!
- Allez-y!
- Mon Dieu!

Example
In our Spanish class, the most popular scenario to depict was a tourist hailing a taxi. The dialogue went something like this:

Tourist: ¡Oye, Taxi!
Taxi Driver: ¡Hola! ¿Adónde Va?
Tourist: Al hotel ¡por favor!

Taxi: Bien: ¡Vámonos!
Tourist: ¡Gracias!

Art Thief

Topic

- Art
- Question words *who, what, where, when,* and *why*

Materials

- Poster print of the stolen artwork
- "Stolen Art!" article taped inside a newspaper, with the story of the theft on the opposite page
- Props for recreating the scene of the crime

Objectives

To learn about an artist in the target culture and the five question words

Instructions

Inform the class that a famous painting has been stolen from a museum in the target country and that someone they know has been accused. The accused can be a student in the class, the class mascot, or a famous person everyone knows. Read aloud the "Stolen Art!" article, which is written in a *who, what, where, when,* and *why* format: "Who: Pepe. What: Stole a Picasso painting from the Madrid Museum," and so on. Then read an account of the morning at the museum, naming the people who came by and giving a funny fact about each one. Pause often to ask the class, "Who ate the apple?" or "Where is the guard?" When you finish, read the story a second time around. This time the class recreates the scene of the crime as you relate the events of the morning. Student volunteers act the parts of characters from the story, pantomiming their actions by pretending to eat apples or look at art. In the end, reveal a crucial new piece of information, and the real art thief is exposed.

Sample "Stolen Art!" article:

¿Quién? Pepe el Dinosaurio (*the stuffed animal mascot in our Spanish class*).

¿Qué? ¡Robó una pintura de Fernando Botero, el pintor más famoso de Colombia!

¿Dónde? En el Museo Colombiano.

¿Cuándo? El 8 de noviembre, a las 11 de la mañana.

¿Por qué? ¡Porque es antipático y un mal dinosaurio!

Note: Make sure to impress on the class that Pepe is not, in fact, a bad dinosaur – he is innocent and his character has been wrongly maligned.

Story of the theft:

Draw on the whiteboard a clock and a few picture frames.

El museo abre a LAS OCHO DE LA MAÑANA cada día. A LAS OCHO hay el guardia y nadie más.

A LAS NUEVE, entra Octavio, un hombre viejo. Octavio trae un papel y un lápiz. Dibuja la pintura de Fernando Botero con su papel y su lápiz.

También A LAS NUEVE DE LA MAÑANA, entra un grupo de estudiantes. Hay catorce estudiantes y una profesora. Los estudiantes miran al arte. Los estudiantes están aburridos.

A LAS NUEVE Y MEDIA, entra Natalia. Natalia come una manzana. Ella come su manzana y mira la pintura de Fernando Botero. El guardia le dice a Natalia que no puede comer la manzana. Natalia se enoja. Ella sale del museo. El guardia come la manzana.

A LAS DIEZ DE LA MAÑANA, sale Octavio con su papel y su lápiz.

A LAS DIEZ Y MEDIA DE LA MAÑANA, salen el grupo de estudiantes y la profesora.

¿Quién todavía está aquí? Nadie salvo el guardia.

Pepe el Dinosaurio entra el museo A LAS DIEZ Y MEDIA DE LA MAÑANA. Pepe camina por el museo mirando el arte. Pepe mira la pintura de Fernando Botero por un largo rato. Pepe hace una llamada por teléfono. Pepe sale A LAS ONCE DE LA MAÑANA.

A LAS ONCE DE LA MAÑANA, la pintura ha desaparecido.

Pepe hizo una llamada por teléfono. *¡El guardia silenciosamente roba la pintura!* Pepe sale a LAS ONCE DE LA MAÑANA.

¡Pepe es inocente!

Word Dice

Topic

- Pronunciation

Materials

- Make or cover 3 dice; 2 should have consonants on all sides and 1 should have only vowels
- Small rewards such as chips or candies at least equal to the number of students (optional)

Objective

To practice pronunciation of simple sounds

Instructions

Students should form two lines. Give the dice to the first two students and tell them to roll the dice at the same time. The first person to make a sound (consonant, vowel, consonant) and pronounce it correctly gets a point or a small reward. Both players move to the back of the line and the next two students move up, and so one. At the end the students with the most points or small rewards get a round of applause.

Example

This card could be pronounced "pod" or "dop."

Vowel Race

Topic

♦ Vowels

Materials

♦ A note card for each student with a vowel written on it

Objective

To practice vowel sounds

Instructions

Make a starting line and have all students line up along it. Give each a different vowel card. Position yourself at the *finish line*. When you call out the sound of a vowel, all the students with that vowel are to run to you. Anyone who runs with the wrong vowel is out. A student who is out can help you by repeating the vowel sound after you call it out.

A Player's Play

Topic

- ◆ Sports
- ◆ Actions
- ◆ Equipment
- ◆ The phrase *I am*

Materials

- ◆ Sports equipment

Objectives

To learn the names of players' positions, equipment, and actions involved in a popular sport from the target culture

Instructions

After introducing the sport, break the students into small groups according to the number of positions available. Assign a different position to each group member. The students act out their position in slow motion. As they pretend to be the player, they must say what position they are playing and what they are doing. For instance, a goalie says, "I am a goalie and I catch the ball." After each student has the chance to say their position within the group, they can switch.

Example

In our Spanish class, we taught the students about soccer. The positions we used were forward, goalie, and defender. The groups were of three students, each taking one of the roles. The student who was a forward said, "I am a forward and I am kicking the ball." The student acting as the defender would block the ball and said, "I am a defender and I block the ball." The student acting as a goalie said, "I am a goalie and I catch the ball." We also added a cultural component by having the students yell, "Gooooooool!" whenever they scored.

At the Game

Topic

- ♦ Sports
- ♦ Actions
- ♦ Chants

Materials

- ♦ Sports chants or cheers
- ♦ Sports equipment

Objectives

To learn the actions involved in playing a sport and be able to cheer for each other using chants from the target culture

Instructions

Tell the students to make a large circle. Have them pass the ball to each other while naming the action they are doing and to whom the ball is being passed. For example, the student kick the ball and say, "Kick to Paula." Whenever the ball is successfully passed five times, the students can simulate the crowd's behavior at an actual game by saying chants from the target culture.

Examples

In our Spanish class, we told the students to pass the soccer ball. When they got used to the game, we had them switch from saying, "Pass to Paula," to saying, "Kick to Paula." When they successfully passed the ball five times, we celebrated by holding each other, jumping, and singing, "¡Olé! ¡Olé! ¡Olé!"

Candy Scouting

Topic

- ♦ Prepositions

Materials

- ♦ 5 written clues (see charts)
- ♦ Snack from the target country

Objectives

To become familiar with prepositions and follow written directions in the target language

Instructions

Make several simple clues before class, such as, "Under the tree" or "Behind the basketball hoop" and hide them outside; the clues should lead from one to another until they finally lead to the location of a snack from the target culture. Divide the class into as many teams as you have clues and explain to the teams should use the clues to find the hidden snack. Take the class outside in a large group, and tell Team 1 the location of the first clue. Have the rest of the students wait while the first team goes out in search of the written clue. When the students find it, they bring it back and give it to Team 2. Team 2 then reads the clue to learn the location of the third clue, and then goes searching for it, and so on through as many teams as you have made clues. Eventually, the last team's clue leads to the candy, which the class can share and enjoy.

Example

Our Japanese class had five teams and five clues, and this number worked well. The first clue read, "Under the tree." The second clue was under the tree, reading, "Behind the basketball hoop." Clue three was behind the basketball hoop, reading, "On the bench," where the fourth clue was, and so forth.

Notes

Make sure you thoroughly explain this activity. It may be helpful to do a demonstration in the classroom to make the students understand that they are working separately in teams but together toward a larger goal with the rest of the class. Make sure the rest of the class stays together while one team goes off in search of a clue, so that only one group at a time is away.

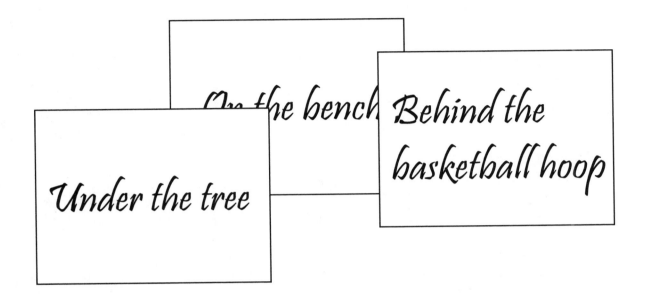

Hello, Good Evening

Topic

♦ Greetings

Materials:

♦ 1 large paper sun

♦ 1 large paper moon

Objective

To become familiar with different greeting customs for different times of the day

Instructions

Hold the paper sun and moon in different ways to depict different times of day. For example, a sun far down on the left of the front of the room represents the morning, up high in the middle of the front of the room represents the afternoon, and down low to the right of the room with a moon held at equal height represents the evening. Holding only the moon up over your head represents night. Use the sun and/or moon to show a certain time of day, and take volunteers to come up and greet you saying, "Good morning," or "Good afternoon," accordingly. Once they understand this, student volunteers choose where to hold the sun and moon. For a more competitive edge, split the class into two teams, and select a volunteer from each team to come up; the first student to greet the group according to the time shown gets a point for the team. This game can be continued until the students feel comfortable with the greetings. The team with the most points in the end wins.

People and Places Match

Topic

- Verb *to be (from)*
- Geography
- Weather
- Seasons
- Cultural symbols

Materials

- 8 *people* cards
- 8 *place* cards
- Tape
- Large map (or overhead transparency) of the target country

Objectives

To expose students to important people of the target culture and to practice the phrase, *I am from*

Instructions

Using 8. 5 × 11–inch paper, create the *people* cards by drawing or printing pictures of five important people of the target culture and writing underneath each image, "I am from [place]." Using 8.5 × 11–inch paper, create a *place* card to match each people card by drawing a simple map of the country with a labeled point marking the corresponding city where the person is from.

Tape the 16 cards facedown on the front board or in a place visible to the entire class. Each student is allowed a turn to flip over two cards. A student who flips over a people card and a place card that matches *wins* those cards and returns to his or her seat. Once all the cards are matched, the card winners return to the front of the class. The teacher asks each winner, "Where are you from?" and the students respond in turn as if they are the famous people on their cards. After saying, "I am from ____," the students point out the specific location on the target country map.

Notes

The following is a variation that aims to familiarize students with seasonal weather in the target country, as well as teach them to associate various cultural symbols with different months of the year. Create a set of memory cards pairing seasons with typical weather for the target country and months with cultural symbols from the target country. In a set of 16 cards, include the four seasons and their corresponding weather patterns (winter/snowy, spring/cloudy, summer/sunny, fall/windy) and 4 months and their corresponding cultural symbols. For example, in a Japanese class the months could be paired with the following cultural symbols:

- April: cherry blossoms
- July: Japanese fan
- October: leaves changing colors
- January: soba noodles

Conversation Circle Walk

Topic
- ♦ Greetings
- ♦ Basic conversation

Materials
- ♦ Target culture music (optional)
- ♦ 1 each of morning sun, afternoon sun, and moon cutouts (optional)
- ♦ Note cards with written greetings or conversational questions (1 per student, optional)

Objectives
To practice greetings and basic conversation in an interactive format

Instructions
Arrange half of the students in a circle facing outward. Arrange the other half in a circle around the first circle, facing inwards. Each student should be facing a person in the other circle (see the example opposite). On your cue, each student in the inner circle says a greeting or question to the partner in the outer circle. The outer partner responds accordingly. After the partners converse, tell the outer circle to rotate to the next partner. Or, instead of simply shifting to the next partner, the outer circle could walk to the sound of music, and when the teacher stops the music, the outer circle stops in front of new partners. The inner circle and outer circle should switch roles or positions after several rotations.

Examples
The conversation can be as simple as the inner circle saying, "Hello!" and the outer circle replying, "Good morning!" You could hold up a cutout of a morning sun, an afternoon sun, or a moon to dictate the outer circle's response of "Good morning," "Good afternoon," or "Good evening." Other conversational topics could be "How are you?" "What is your name?" "How old are you?" "What is your favorite animal?" or "What time is it?"

Notes
A variation on this activity could be to give each inner circle student a note card with a specific greeting or question written on it. For example, a third of the cards could ask, "What is your name?" A third could ask, "How old are you?" The final third could ask, "How are you?" In this format, the outer circle students can have different conversations when the circle rotates. Do not allow the inner circle students to read directly from the note cards (especially after a few rounds), but allow students to use them as reminders of their greeting or question.

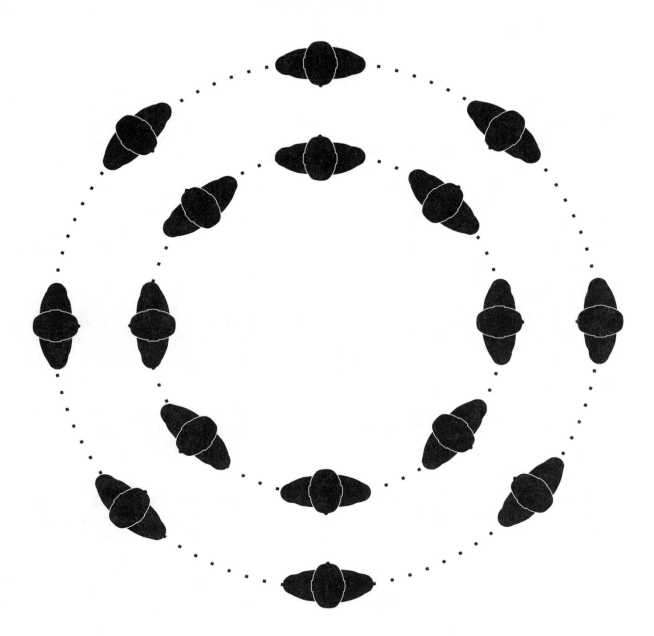

All Write!

Topic

- ◆ Writing
- ◆ Spelling

Materials

- ◆ Plain white paper (1 sheet for each student)
- ◆ Markers
- ◆ White board

Objectives

To learn how to write in the target language, especially if the writing system is different but also in terms of orthography

Instructions

Distribute a sheet of blank paper to each person in the class. Write a few words in the target language on the whiteboard and have the students copy them onto the white paper a few times to familiarize themselves with how they are written. Then split the class into four teams and call on a member of each team to come up to the whiteboard. Say one of the words. The first student to write the word correctly and sit down on the floor wins a point for the team; but if the student sits down and it is written incorrectly, a point is subtracted from the team's score. The team with the most points in the end wins.

Note

This activity is ideal for languages that do not use the Roman alphabet; specifically for the Asian languages such as Japanese or Chinese with logographic writing systems, this activity gives the students a taste of the *cool* different way to write things without going in depth into the writing system.

10

Personal Descriptions

Passports

Topic

♦ Descriptive adjectives

Materials

♦ Passport worksheets

Objectives

To learn about the logistics of traveling to another country and to learn to give personal descriptions in the target language

Instructions

You can make passport worksheets using 8.5 × 11–inch paper. Write at the top of the worksheets, "The passport of ___." Underneath, list various descriptive adjectives, using the target language, in paired opposites such as boy/girl, tall/short, young/old, and so forth (see chart).

Students choose the characteristics on the passport that best describe them and copy them onto the appropriate lines. When they finish, they line up by the door with their passports. You act as the border guard and check off each passport as students step outside across the *border* between America and the target country. On the other side of the door, another teacher or student may stand dressed as the president, king, or leader of that country to greet students as they pass through.

Example

Our Spanish class traveled to Panama and on arrival greeted the Panamanian president (another teacher wearing a sash and a mustache). This gave students the opportunity to practice the greetings we taught them earlier. The president greeted them with, "¿Cómo estás?" while the student responded with the more formal, "¿Cómo está?"

El pasaporte de <u>Pepe</u>

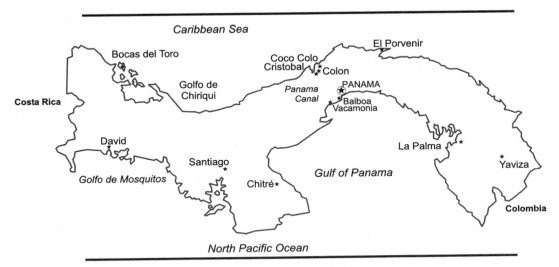

¿Cómo eres tú?

Chico/Chica:

_____ chico _____

Viejo/Joven:

_____ joven _____

Color de Ojos:

_____ azul _____

Color de Pelo

Rubio/Moreno:

_____ rubio _____

**Alto/Bajo:

_____ alto _____

Artista (sí/no):

_____ no _____

Simpático/Antipático:

_____ simpático _____

Divertido/Serio:

_____ divertido _____

Tímido/Extrovertido:

_____ extrovertido _____

Deportista (sí/no):

_____ sí _____

Inteligente (sí/no):

_____ sí _____

X_____Pepe_____

Fecha: El __ de _____ de 2006

La firma de la maestra aqui

** Si eres una CHICA, eres alta/baja, simpática/antipática, etc.

People Bingo

Topic

♦ Descriptive adjectives

Materials

♦ Bingo cards

Objectives

To learn to ask and tell others about oneself

Instructions

To make bingo cards, divide a piece of paper into six or more squares. In each square, write two to three adjectives, one of which specifies a gender. For example, one square reads, "blonde, short girl," another reads, "outgoing boy," and another reads, "Dark-haired, athletic girl." Photocopy this Bingo card to provide one for each student.

Within a certain time limit, students move around the room finding classmates who match the descriptions on their Bingo cards, and asking them to initial the square they match. Students can practice simple questions like "Are you athletic?" "Are you outgoing?" The winner is the student who is first to get all her squares initialed by classmates. Those who speak English during the game are eliminated.

Chico extrovertido	Chica rubia, baja	Chica morena, atlética
Chicaa rtística	Chico moreno, inteligente	Chico alto, timido
Chico rubio, alto	Chicab aja	Chico artístico

You're Up, Stand Up

Topic

   ♦ Verb *to be*
   ♦ Verb *to have*
   ♦ Descriptive words
   ♦ Colors, Clothing

Objective

   To understand the verbs *to be* and *to have* by applying them to personal descriptions

Instructions

   Have all the students stand in front of their chairs with their eyes closed. Once everyone is settled, begin to describe a student in the class using sentences beginning with, "You are…" and "You have…." Whenever the students hear a description that does not apply to them, they must sit down. As a result, every student must very carefully listen to the teacher to gage whether or not the description applies. The game ends when only one student is left standing. If that student meets all of the descriptions stated by the teacher, he or she must then tell the class "I am…" or "I have…" so the class can confirm that this was the student described.

Example

   In our Spanish class, we started out with very general statements such as, "You have brown hair," and "You are a girl." Once the class was narrowed down to a few students, we used statements involving clothing to eliminate the remaining students such as, "You have a brown shirt," or "You have blue shoes." This is a great way to teach the students about clothing and color vocabulary in a competitive environment.

Notes

   Here is an alternate ending to the game, which puts students on the spot by allowing them to answer questions about physical descriptions and then portray emotions. Once the group standing consists of only five or ten students, ask a quiz question about yourself or another student. For example, "Am I blond or brown-haired?" or "Is he tall or short?" The first person in the group to give the correct answer proceeds to the front of the class. Ask another quiz question. The first person in the remaining group to give the correct answer also proceeds to the front of the class. Give the pair of students a personality word to act out for the class and provide them with props if necessary. For example, the students could be given the word *funny* and pretend to whisper a joke to one another and then break out laughing. Then, allow students in the audience to guess the personality word.

Guess Who

Topic

♦ Hobbies

Materials

♦ People poster

♦ 1 set of hobby cards for each group depicting and naming all the hobbies on the poster board

♦ 1 envelope for each set of hobby cards

Objectives

To learn the phrase *he likes* and *she likes* as well as vocabulary for various hobbies

Instructions

Choose six famous people from the target culture for this game. Divide a poster board into approximately six columns (equal to the number of groups of students). At the top of each column, write the phrase "[Famous person] likes…." In each column, list the activities the person likes. Hobbies can be repeated in different columns, but each column should contain the number of hobbies equal to the number of students per group. For example, if the person is a famous painter, painting should be one of his hobbies.

Divide the students into groups. Describe the poster to the students and have them repeat each person's hobbies. Then secretly tell each group of students the name of one celebrity and give them an envelope containing a set of hobby cards. Have them work together to distinguish what their person likes to do, using the information on the poster board. They should return the leftover cards to the envelope. (To make sure the kids understand what they are doing, you could have an extra *person* on the poster and show them what to do). One group begins with its members standing up one at a time and telling the class one hobby that their person enjoys, using the phrase, "He [or she] likes…." The other students use the poster to guess who the group describes. The game proceeds with each group presenting the hobbies of its designated famous person.

Note

A variation of the game can be applied to teach about the Mexican celebration of Day of the Dead. Here, the famous people are famous Mexicans who have died. Instead of just giving the groups a person to present, secretly tell them they are part of the famous person's family. Next they make a traditional shrine for their dead family member using the things he or she liked while living. You could either give the students a *shrine,* which could be as simple as a shoe box, or you could have them make one, perhaps with a shoe box and tissue paper. They can simply place the hobby cards onto the shrine, draw their own pictures, or make some other visual representation of the hobbies. Groups still tell the other groups what their family member liked and the other groups would guess what family they are.

Pen Pals

Topic
- Description

Materials
- Blank paper, blank cards, or a template

Objectives
To practice describing oneself in a letter format

Instructions
To make a template, write a letter with spaces for the students to fill in. Give the students options to fill in the spaces such as, "I have blue/green/brown/black eyes," or leave the spaces blank.

Give the students blank cards or templates. After the students finish filling in their cards, deliver them to another language class so those students can write back, or have the two halves of the classroom switch their letters. For a variation of this activity, have the students write to an imaginary student their age in the target country. Then you could reply to their letters, pretending to be that student. Or better yet, have e-mail correspondences with a class of students in a country that speaks the target language and foster a cultural exchange.

Example

Hello		well
———— My name is _____. How are you? I'm doing …	————
Goodbye		poorly

I have __black__ hair, and __blue__ eyes.

__brown__	__green__
__red__	__brown__
blond	black

Tell Me About It

Topic

◆ Adjectives

Materials

◆ Note cards with pictures of nouns on the back

◆ Microphone

◆ Timer (optional)

Objective

To learn to describe nouns using adjectives

Instructions

Split the class into two teams. Simulate a game show atmosphere, with the host (teacher) using a microphone and the students applauding loudly between rounds. Select a member of the first team to come up, take a card, look at the picture on the back without showing it to the team, and describe it to the teammates with a variety of adjectives. If the team guesses the correct noun, they get a point. If not, the other team can try to guess. To make the game go faster or be more competitive, each round can be on a timer (a kitchen timer works well or just watch the clock). After the first team's time is up, the play moves to the next team. Continue until all the cards have been used. The team with the most points in the end wins.

Example

Our Japanese class used nouns such as *pencil* (long, yellow, thin) and *snow* (cold, white).

11

Weather, Travel, and Geography

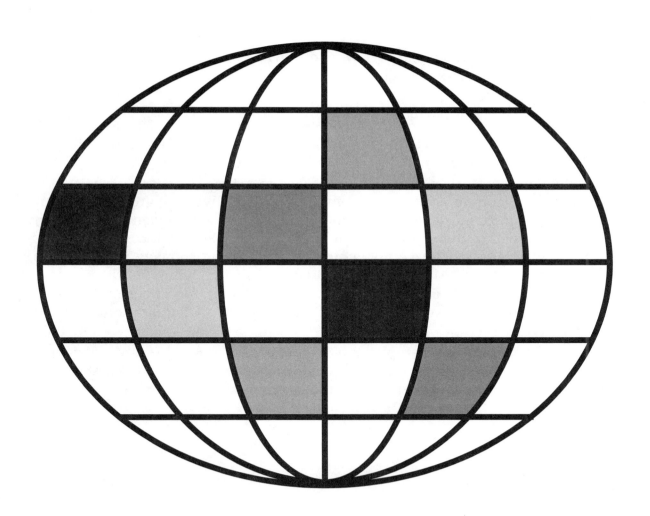

Geography Theater

Topic

- ◆ Geography
- ◆ Animal vocabulary
- ◆ Environmental vocabulary
- ◆ Weather

Materials

- ◆ Geography clue cards (one for every 4 to 5 students)

Objective

To learn vocabulary associated with different geographical regions within a country speaking the target language

Instructions

To make the clue cards, on 3 × 5–inch note cards, either draw pictures of or write the words for various items found within different geographical regions, such as the jungle, the ocean, the forest, the desert, the mountains, the beach, etc.

Gather students into groups of four or five depending on the size of the class or the number of geographical regions being performed. Give each group a clue card with words or pictures, depending on the students' level of proficiency, of different things found within their geographical location. For example, for a group acting out *The Jungle,* pass out a card with pictures of, or words for, monkey, trees, flowers, rain, snake, and so on. Allow each group time to practice acting out the words or images on their clue cards, then call them up group by group to perform for their classmates. After their performance, the class must guess what location the group was portraying.

On the facing page are examples of two types of geography clue cards for a Spanish class. Both are for a group given the jungle or *la jungla* however, the first is in list format for more advanced students and the second is in picture format.

Cue Card:
La Jungla

1. El Mono
2. El Serpiente
3. La Lluvia
4. La Flor
5. El Árbol

Cue Card:
La Jungla

Weather Alert!

Topic

- Weather
- Seasons

Materials

- Weather signs (one for every student)

Objectives

To gain an understanding of the four seasons and the types of weather commonly associated with each season

Instructions

Weather signs are popsicle sticks with pictures consisting of a type of weather taped to the top. Make sure to have enough different weather signs so that each season is represented by at least two different types of weather, for example, rain and wind for fall or snow and ice for winter.

Divide the class into groups of 14 or a similar number depending on the size of the class and how many types of weather you want to incorporate. Then, distribute the different popsicle stick *weather signs* to the students, making sure that for each group the four seasons are fully represented, containing the two types of weather associated with each. For example, winter is represented by students holding up snow and ice signs, whereas spring is represented by students holding rain and cloud signs. Before the game can begin, designate a student to be the *weather watchperson*, the person responsible for calling out a season to the class. The game begins when the weather watchperson looks out the classroom window and calls out a season. The first group to hold up all the correct weather signs used to represent that season wins. The game can be made more complicated by having the weather watchperson call out a season, and having the first team to hold up all of the weather signs associated with the *following* season win.

Notes

Make it clear to the students that for the activity only the two specified types of weather you have stated can be used to illustrate a season as some types of weather such as rain or sun can be found in more than one season.

The Weatherman

Topic

♦ Weather

♦ Days of the week

Materials

♦ Paper mustache and tape

♦ Weather props such as an umbrella, a scarf, and sunglasses (optional)

Objectives

To practice weather vocabulary and days of the week

Instructions

In this game students track changes in the weather over the course of 7 days. To begin, a student goes to the front of the room and puts on the weatherman's mustache. Introduce the Monday Weatherman to the class. Whisper a weather vocabulary word to the student to act out using props or total physical response (TPR) actions such as catching snowflakes on his or her tongue to represent *snowing* and fanning for *sunny*. The other students guess the weather the Monday Weatherman is depicting. Then a new weatherman acts out Tuesday's weather. The class repeats this for each day of the week and can prognosticate as many weeks as you desire.

Note

To vary the game a little, students may draw on the board instead of acting out the vocabulary.

I Spy Story

Topic

- Travel
- Scenery
- Geography
- Story telling

Materials

- *I Spy* book
- Visual representations of each object you spy

Objective

To learn the vocabulary associated with a setting from the target country

Instructions

To make the *I Spy* book, first decide what kind of imaginary travel you and your class are taking, such as rowing down a river, climbing a mountain, driving through a city or country, and so forth. On the first page, spy an object that you would see in your setting. With each subsequent page, add an object after repeating the previous object(s). On each page, draw all the objects seen thus far (see example).

After the students have gathered around you, read the story once while pointing to the pictures in the book. Next, read the book while holding up the objects as you *spy* them in the book. Then have the students act as if they were traveling across the mountain, down the river, or whatever setting you choose. After they say in unison (on your cue), "I spy with my little eye," or the idiomatic equivalent, hold up an object and have them shout out what they see. For example, if the students are pretending to hike, row, or drive, and say in unison, "I spy with my little eye," hold up something depicted in the story, such as the visual representation of a tree. The students finish their phrase by shouting out, "A tree!" The class continues traveling, shouting out the "I spy" line when you hold up different objects with which they are to finish the line. Next, give the objects (the visual representations) to some children and read the story again, pointing to them as a cue to the class to shout the object's name. For example, on page 3 of the example book in the following text, you read, "I spy with my little eye a…" and cue the student holding the sun to hold it up and shout, "Sun!" Continue reading the page, "and a…" and cue the student with the bird to hold up and shout, "Bird!" Make sure many students get the chance to hold one of the objects.

Example

Page 1: "I'm Pepe. I am rowing my boat to an island."
Page 2: "I spy with my little eye a sun."
Page 3: "I spy with my little eye a sun and a bird."
Page 4: "I spy with my little eye a sun, a bird, and a fish."

Page 5: "I spy with my little eye a sun, a bird, a fish, and a tree."

Page 6: "I spy with my little eye a sun, a bird, a fish, a tree, and an island!"

For more repetition, add pages for the boy's return trip in which he sees less and less. For example, first the boy could say "I spy with my little eye a sun, a bird, a fish, and a tree." The next page, he can only see the sun, bird, and the fish. The next page he can just see the sun and bird. And finally, he only sees the sun.

Theatrical Weather Map

Topic

♦ Weather

♦ Geography

Materials

♦ A large map of the target country with drawings depicting the weather (small sun, rain cloud, etc.) next to a few major cities

Objectives

To become familiar with phrases to describe the weather and with the basic geography of the target country

Instructions

Split the class into as many teams as there are cities and weather patterns and secretly assign each team a city. The teams either prepare their own TPR motions for the weather pattern or use the ones learned earlier in class to act out their weather pattern in front of the other teams. Team 1 acts out the weather in front of the class as Team 2 guesses the city and type of weather Team 1 is depicting. Teams receive 1 point for the correct city and 1 point for the correct weather pattern. If they cannot correctly name either, the response is opened to the whole class, and the team that answers fastest wins the point. Next, Team 2 would come up, with Team 3 providing responses, and so on, until all teams have a chance to act. The team with the most points in the end wins.

Example

Our Japanese class used five major cities in Japan (Tokyo, Kyoto, Sapporo, Osaka, and Fukuoka) to practice the weather patterns *snowy, sunny, windy, rainy,* and *cloudy.* Five weather patterns is a good number, because any more may become overly complicated or time consuming.

Kyoto

Tenki yôhô

JAPAN

Sapporo

Tokyo

Kyoto

Osaka

Fukuoka

What's Weather?

Topic

- Weather
- Seasons

Materials

- Weather equipment (e.g., umbrella, sunglasses, scarf, etc.)
- Blindfold

Objective

To practice the names of different weather systems, such as hot, cold, rainy, and so on

Instructions

Introduce the weather systems using TPR. Separate the students into two teams. Have each team choose a representative and a helper to go to the front of the class. Each helper blindfolds the team representative. When the representatives' eyes are covered, get a prop that is specific to a type of weather. For example, an umbrella could be used for rain. Give the helpers a sign to take off the blindfold. Show the representatives the prop. The first representative to name the weather and act it out using the correct TPR gets a point for the team. Choose a new representative after each round.

Examples

In our Spanish class, we used a specific TPR to describe each weather system. Some of the TPR we used was that we fanned ourselves for hot weather, shivered for cold weather, and wiggled our fingers and moved our hands up and down for rainy weather.

Note

This game can also be applied to seasons.

Train Tour

Topic

- ◆ Travel vocabulary
- ◆ Geography
- ◆ Monuments

Materials

- ◆ Map of the target country
- ◆ Visuals of various monuments

Objectives

To become familiar with the major monuments and the basic geography of the target country, as well as to experience train travel within that country

Instructions

Take the class outside (or circle the room) and have the students line up as a train with you at the head. Chug around the room in a circle, perhaps while singing an easy train song, and simulate normal announcements made on that country's trains. Then stop the train, and tell everyone to face the middle, where you become the tour guide. Hold up a picture of a major monument in the city, and have the class repeat the name of the monument, plus that language's equivalent of "Ooh! Ah!" or "Wow!" Then get back on the train and travel to the other destinations to see the other monuments. When the trip is complete, have the students draw postcards of the monuments in the various cities. For more advanced classes, students could also write on the postcard about what they saw.

Example

Our Japanese class's train stopped through six Japanese cities, with a major monument in each. These were the Tokyo Tower in Tokyo, the Golden Pavilion Temple in Kyoto, the Osaka Castle in Osaka, the A-bomb Dome in Hiroshima, Mount Fuji in Shizuoka, and the large Buddha statue in Nara. The *conductor* made announcements when the train was approaching the station, such as, "Presently, we are arriving at Tokyo Station, Tokyo Station," or "The next stop is Osaka Station, Osaka Station." Even if students do not understand these full announcements, it gives a more authentic feel to the whole journey.

Note

This game could also be played by traveling to the country by plane first, simulating what it would be like to be on an airline of the target country. Instead of visiting monuments, visit different natural locations such as mountains, oceans, or lakes. To incorporate adjectives, instead of having the students exclaim, "Wow!" They could also exclaim, "How big/wide/long/green," and so on, depending on the location being viewed.

Quick Draw

Topic

- Review
- Weather
- Seasons
- Animals
- Foods
- Transportation

Materials

- White board, black board, or easel
- 1 drawing utensil

Objective

To review vocabulary

Instructions

Choose one volunteer to secretly tell a vocabulary word, perhaps by writing it out on a piece of paper. The student illustrates the vocabulary word on the board. The first person to correctly guess the vocabulary word is the next artist. Continue the game in this fashion. To make this game more competitive, split the class into two teams. The teams take turns drawing for their teammates and a correct guess by their teammates earn their team a point.

Notes

This activity can be used with any vocabulary that is illustratable.

Geographical Musical Chairs

Topic

- Geographical feature vocabulary
- Verb *to be (located)*

Materials

- Images of geographical features (on 8.5 × 11–inch paper)
- Tape
- Music from the target culture

Objectives

To test knowledge of geographical feature vocabulary and the use of *to be (located)*

Instructions

Tape the images of geographical features faceup on several different desks. When the music starts, the students walk aimlessly around the classroom while the teacher removes one or more desk chairs. When the music stops, students try to find a desk with a chair to sit in. The students who do not find a chair are out of the game. One at a time, ask the students at the *geographical* desks, "Where are you?" The student must respond correctly to stay in the game or be out. For example, if a student is sitting at a desk with an image of the mountains taped to it, the correct response is, "I am in the mountains." Start the music again, removing the proper number of chairs and continue with as many rounds as time permits.

Example

Our five geographical features were the mountains, the river, the ocean, the desert, and the forest. We taped a large photo of each of these on different desks.

Note

If the chairs and desks are one unit, the teacher can place an *X* note on the desks that are *removed* from the game. Also, this game can get very loud and chaotic, so remind the students to walk slowly and carefully when the music stops.

12

Review
(Any Topic)

Surprise Party

Topic

- Holidays
- Birthdays
- Songs
- Food
- Games

Materials

- Materials to decorate the classroom for a birthday party specific to the target language (e.g., streamers in colors specific to a flag from the target language, balloons, paper for posters on which the students can write culturally relevant well-wishes, festive music, etc.)
- Letter-sized pieces of paper for each student
- Colored pens, pencils, or crayons (enough so that each student may use some)

Objectives

To learn vocabulary associated with parties and how to sing happy birthday

Instructions

The activity celebrates the birthday of an imaginary guest from the target culture. Begin by telling the class that they must prepare for the guest's surprise birthday party. Divide the class into four groups, each of which is assigned a different task in planning the surprise party. The first group is in charge of food and must decide what food from the target language they want at the party. After they have done so, ask them to draw the food on letter-sized paper. Tell the second group to choose gifts to give the surprise guest and have them draw the gifts on letter-sized paper. The third group is in charge of decorations and must decorate the classroom with culturally specific decorations for the guest. The fourth group is in charge of making birthday cards. Each member of the group creates a card in the target language for the birthday guest. When all the groups have finished, the mystery guest *arrive*. Have the class sing a culturally relevant "Happy Birthday" song to the birthday guest. To end, have each group share what they created for the party.

Note

To make the party more enjoyable for the students, bring something edible and culturally relevant for them to eat as a treat during the party. The birthday guest for the party could range from a stuffed animal to surprise visitor.

Silent Movie Stars

Topic

♦ Any

Materials

♦ A list of approximately 10 vocabulary words that students can pantomime

Objective

To actively review vocabulary

Instructions

Separate students into four equal-sized groups and instruct each to send a member to the front of the room. Whisper to those students the first vocabulary word on the list. Then, on your signal, all four run back to their tables to act out the word without speaking. The first student from each group to correctly guess the word runs back to you and (quietly) repeats it to you. If is correct, give the student the next word to act out for the group. The first team to guess all the vocabulary words wins.

Notes

You can play this game to practice the names of animals, emotions, and a variety of other vocabulary.

Shout Out

Topic

♦ Any

Materials

♦ Pictures or other visual representations of the vocabulary

Objective

Vocabulary review

Instructions

Divide the class into two lines facing you, and instruct the first student in each line to step forward. Count to three, encouraging all the students to join in, and on "three," hold up a picture. The first of the two students to name it wins a point for the team. Then both return to the back of the lines and the next two students step forward. Cycle through until all pictures are named.

Example

Our Spanish class played this game to review colors, days of the week, numbers (for which we held up fingers rather than pictures), and various other words the students had learned. We had the native Spanish speakers keep track of points for each team. Students enjoyed creating team names beforehand and doing a quick team cheer before the game.

Note

It's a good idea to go over pictures a few times if students have trouble with them, as well as to repeat the easier words, because the students often become excited when they can rattle off a word they know.

Go Fish

Topic

+ Colors, Numbers
+ Weather
+ Days of the week
+ School supplies
+ Animals

Materials

+ A deck of cards for each group (perhaps note cards cut in half), colored a solid color on one side

Objectives

To practice colors

Instructions

Each group should have multiples of 4 cards of each color. Plan on groups of five students; give each student 5 cards with a draw pile of 12 or 16 cards. Pass out approximately five cards to each student and give each group a draw pile. Instruct them to take turns asking a group member if she has a card of a certain color (the asker must have that color card, and the student who is asked must give up such card if she has it). If the student receives the card he asked for, he can continue asking individual members in the group for cards until someone says, "No." Then he picks a card from the draw pile and play moves to the student on the left. When a student has four cards of one color, she puts this match face up on the table in front of her. The game ends when one student in the group is out of cards.

Notes

The rules for Go Fish are very flexible and can be manipulated to fit the number of students in the class and the length of time available. You can also have the students practice numbers by playing Go Fish with a regular deck of cards or make decks using any other vocabulary such as school supplies, weather, animals, or days of the week.

Hop To It

Topic

- Numbers
- School supplies
- Animals
- Geography
- Letters

Materials

- Either butcher paper and markers or sidewalk chalk (if the class has access to cement or asphalt)
- Hopscotch

Objective

To become very comfortable with numbers (or other objects)

Instructions

Prepare by making hopscotch squares on paper or on the sidewalk. Make each single box a number or alternatively draw a picture in each box. Make sure to give the horizontal boxes the same number or object (see chart).

After taping down the butcher paper or drawing the hopscotch squares with sidewalk chalk, have the students form a line at the start of hopscotch. Instruct them to jump across the hopscotch, announcing what they are landing on as they jump into each box. When learning numbers, it works well to draw an easy hopscotch with ascending numbers, a medium difficulty hopscotch with the numbers descending, and a tricky one with the order of numbers jumbled. Having more than one set of hopscotch squares also lets more students participate at once.

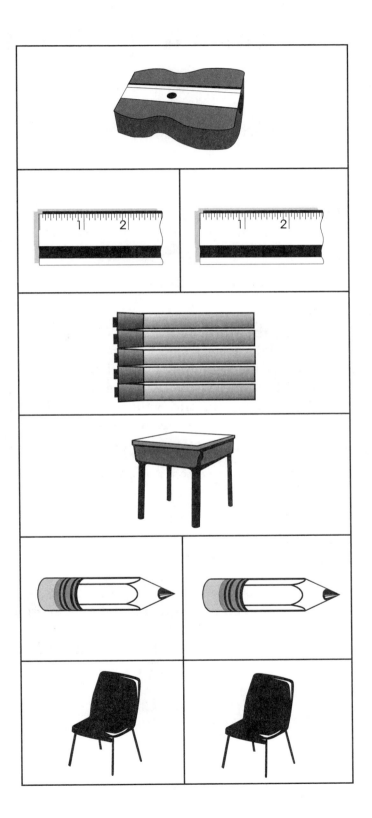

Chant It up, Sit on Down

Topic

♦ Colors

♦ Days of the week

♦ Months

♦ Body parts

Materials

♦ A number of chairs equaling the number of students minus 1

Objective

To practice vocabulary by chanting

Instructions

After teaching the students the song or chant, arrange the chairs in a circle (see charts for additional arrangements). Have the students chant while walking or dancing around the chairs. When they finish the chant, each student tries to sit in a chair; whoever is left standing is out. Take one chair out of the circle. Have the students stand up and begin chanting and walking around the chairs again. Repeat until there is a winner. The *out* students stand to the side and continue chanting the song.

Example

A Spanish chant for the days of the week is as follows:

Lunes, martes, miércoles, tres;

Jueves, viernes, sábado, seis;

Domingo, siete, y sabe ya

Que la semana completa está.

Note

To make the game go more quickly, take away more than one chair each round. You can also take players out of the game if they are not chanting. On the facing page are two bird's eye view options with six students playing.

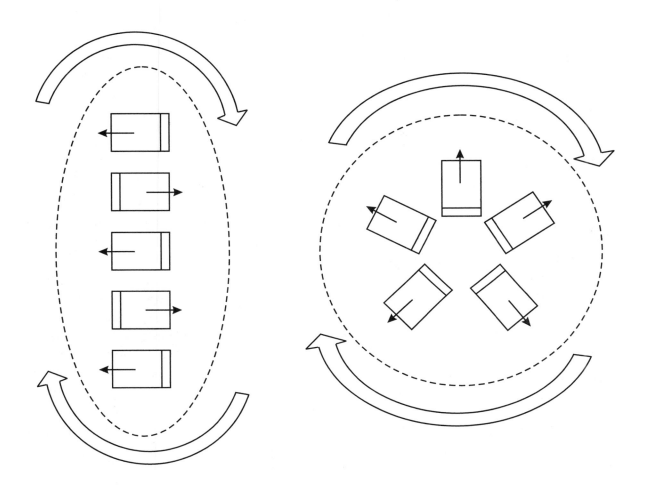

Battleship

Topic

- ◆ Review

Materials

- ◆ 2 posters (see instructions)

Objective

To review previously learned vocabulary and phrases

Instructions

On each poster draw a grid with the rows labeled with letters A through approximately E, and the columns labeled with numbers 1 through approximately 5. Each square on the grid contains a question (see sample). Cover the questions with Post-it notes and put smaller Post-its in the corners of the squares. The squares with a part of a battleship have Xs under the smaller Post-its.

Divide the classroom into two teams. Hang up the two posters on the wall. Call on one student from Team 1. That player picks a square by saying the corresponding number and letter, "A-1 please." Remove the Post-it note covering the question and read the question. If the student answers correctly, remove the smaller Post-it to see if the student hit a battleship. If the student does not answer correctly, leave the question uncovered, but do not remove the smaller Post-it. Now, it is Team 2's turn. The player can either try to answer a different question or a question a previous student missed. The large Post-its cover the questions to challenge students, so they do not just pick questions to which they know the answer. A team wins when one of its players correctly answers the last question needed to sink the battleship. For instance, if the battleship spans three questions (A1, A2, and A3), and questions A1 and A2 have already been answered correctly, the first team to correctly answer A3 wins the game.

Examples

Team 1's poster could look something like the following chart. Team 2 could have the same questions and battleships in different positions on the chart.

Notes

You can add a cultural aspect to this game by searching for something other than battleships (like an animal in the forest or a ship of a famous explorer).

	1	2	3	4	5
A	What's the weather? [snowflake]	I have to go to the ____." [toilet]	What is this called? [dolphin]	What is this called? [orange]	What is this called? [pyramid]
B	What is this called? [hand]	What is this called? [snake]	Count from 1 to 10.	What is this called? [jacket]	Respond: What is your name?
C	What color is this? [yellow]	What is this called? [elephant]	What's the weather? [umbrella]	Respond: How are you?	What color is this? [blue]
D	What is this called? [bird]	What is this called? [shirt] (x)	What is this called? [knee] (x)	What color is this? [black] (x)	What part of your body do your pants go on?
E	What color is this? [green]	What is this called? [socks]	What is this called? [tree]	What color is this? [red]	What's the weather? [sun]

Drama Competition

Topic

- Legends
- Performance
- Commenting
- Object review

Materials

- A book with illustrations or a picture book
- Props
- 3 sets of index cards with the words *good, very good,* and *excellent* written on them

Objectives

To review vocabulary words and to practice using the words *good, very good,* and *excellent,* while hearing tales from the target culture

Instructions

A well-known story can be turned into a simplified picture book by drawing the major events of the story on poster-sized pages. Make sure to draw pictures that focus on the keywords you would like your students to learn. You can include text, but it is not necessary.

Slowly tell the students the story using the picture book. Focus on desired keywords by using TPR. After the students have heard the story once or twice, select three volunteers to be judges. They each receive the index cards. Then tell the students they are competing in a drama competition. Separate the class into two groups, excluding the three judges. Give the groups approximately 2 minutes to plan their performance of the story. They should narrate and act out the story according to the picture book. They can use the picture book and any props available. While they are acting, take note of any keywords and total physical response (TPR) the students use. Groups get a point for each keyword they use during their performance. After each performance, the judges give a score of *good, very good,* and *excellent.* Assign 1 point for *good,* 2 points for *very good,* and 3 points for *excellent.* The final score is the sum of the judges' scores plus the sum of the keyword points. The group with the highest score wins the drama competition.

Example

In our Spanish class, we made a picture book of the story of the Llorona. To emphasize the keywords, we used props and TPR and had the students repeat the words.

Examples of the beginning and the end of the story of the Llorona, with narration are on the facing page.

Note

It can be helpful to give the students lots of props. Even if the objects are unrelated to the story, the students tend to find a good way to incorporate them. Also, if there are more students than characters, remind them that they can portray the setting or certain objects using the TPR they learn.

Narration:
La Llorona era una mujer muy bella.
(The Llorona was a beautiful woman.)

Narration:
La Llorona llora al lado del río por sus hijos.
(The Llorona cries by the river for her children.)

Name That Price!

Topic

- ◆ Numbers
- ◆ Currency
- ◆ Review of objects

Materials

- ◆ Objects previously learned
- ◆ Index cards with the prices of objects on them

Objectives

To review the names of items and learn to say their prices with currency from the target culture

Instructions

Separate the class into three or four groups and tell each group to choose a representative. Present an object. Give the participants 10 seconds to talk to their group and write an estimated price of the object. When the time is up, have each representative say the price the group selected. After the last representative has guessed, present the actual price. The group that guesses the closest to the actual price without going over gets a point. Go through several rounds with different representatives and different items. In the end, the group with the most points wins.

Example

In our Spanish class, we used clothing items and school supplies. These are items that we had taught in previous lessons, so the students were familiar with the objects.

Notes

If the class is young or has trouble with multiplication, the currency should transfer directly (i.e., $1 = 1 peso). If they can be challenged, use real currency value rounded to the nearest whole number (i.e., if $1.00 = 9.75 pesos, use $1 = 10 pesos).

Heartthrob

Topic

- Vocabulary review
- Sentences

Materials

- 8.5 × 11–inch pictures of vocabulary words
- 2 heart masks
- A shoebox

Objectives

To recognize visual representations of previously taught vocabulary words and to practice using them in complete sentences

Instructions

A heart mask is made by cutting a heart out of an 8.5 × 11–inch piece of red construction paper and pasting a popsicle stick at the bottom so that it can be held.

Fold all the pictures in half and put them in the shoebox. Divide the class into two groups and ask each group to choose a representative. Randomly choose a picture from the box and show it to the class. The first group representative to raise a hand gives the team the chance to answer. At the direction of the captain, the whole group says the name of the vocabulary word in the target language in a complete sentence using the phrase, "This is…" to get 1 point. If the group says it using TPR, they receive 2 points. If the group answers incorrectly, subtract 1 point from their score. The group with the most points in the end wins.

Example

In our Spanish class, we added a cultural review to the lesson by letting the representative from the winning team perform a sacrificial killing on the opposing team's representative using the heart masks. The cultural review focused on the Aztecs who were known to do sacrificial killings. To perform the ritual, the losing representative holds the heart mask over his or her chest. The winning representative takes it, as the losing representative pretends to die. In the event that a representative is sacrificed, another student from the team becomes the new representative and begins a new round.

Note

The students can challenge each other to a duel, draw, sword fight, or can behead each other instead of doing the Aztec sacrificial rituals.

Tic-Tac-Toe

Topic

- ◆ Vocabulary review
- ◆ Number review
- ◆ Letter review

Materials

- ◆ Printouts or drawings of vocabulary words on 8.5 × 11–inch papers with numbers on the back
- ◆ Chalkboard or whiteboard
- ◆ Tape

Objective

To review previously taught vocabulary words and numbers

Instructions

Draw the outline for tic-tac-toe on the board, and in each square tape the paper with the picture of the vocabulary word face down so that only the number is showing. Divide the class into two groups, Group X and Group O. Flip a coin to decide which group goes first. The students work within their groups to decide which box to pick by saying the corresponding letter or number. When the box is chosen, the paper is flipped over and the picture is revealed. The students have 10 seconds to say the corresponding vocabulary word as a group to win an X or an O in the box they choose. If the group does not correctly name the vocabulary word, the opposing team's letter is written in their box. The first group to get their three Xs or Os in a line wins.

Notes

To challenge students, the numbers written can be two- or three-digit numbers. The students should have to say the correct name of the number to choose the box. Letters can also be used instead of numbers.

Name Me!

Topic

- Vocabulary review
- Number review

Materials

- Vocabulary cards
- Small pieces of paper with numbers corresponding to the vocabulary cards
- A hat (or bowl)

Objective

To review previously taught vocabulary words and numbers

Instructions

To make the vocabulary cards, paste large pictures (from the Internet or magazines) of vocabulary words on one side of an 8.5 × 11–inch page, then write a number on the reverse side of the page. Each page should have a different number.

Fold the small, numbered papers and put them in the hat. Split the class into four or five groups. Tape the vocabulary cards to the board with only the numbers showing. Approach each group and ask a member to pick a number out of the hat. The number picked corresponds with the number on the card and the amount of points the group can potentially receive for correctly naming the vocabulary card. When the card is flipped over, the group must decide on the name and say it correctly in unison to receive the points. Continue this until all the groups have the chance to guess a vocabulary word. The groups have 15 seconds to answer in the first round. In each additional round they have 5 seconds less to answer. In the end, the group with the most points wins.

Example

In our Spanish class, we used this game for any type of vocabulary. The vocabulary ranged from emotions to animals.

Puzzle Scramble

Topic

♦ Vocabulary review

Materials

♦ Photocopies of the puzzle sheet (one for each student)

Objectives

To match written vocabulary words with pictures of the review words

Instructions

The puzzle works as follows: the piece of paper is divided into a 5 × 7–inch grid of squares. On each of the 4 insides of the square is written a different word or picture. Across the line in the next square is the corresponding picture or word definition. The entire sheet lines up so that every side has a matching word and picture (see chart).

The students are given an 8.5 × 11–inch puzzle sheet. The students cut up the grid, mix up the squares, and put them back together so all the words and pictures match. Whoever does it quickest and correctly wins.

Notes

Allow enough time for the students to cut out the pieces and work on the puzzle, because this can take a while. If they cut out the pieces at home the night before, they may try to color code the puzzle to make it easier (we saw this happen in our Japanese class).

tamago	yubiwa	empitsu
		ie
yen	kumo	hi
te	kutsu	tori
densha	tokei	hebi
sakana	osushi	hana
yama	hashi	ame
makura	hoshi	ringo
ki	uchiwa	mushi
uwagi	terebi	juusu
	karaoke	neko
		zubon

SLAP the Vocab!

Topic

♦ Review

Materials

♦ Visual representations of vocabulary words, which can easily be taped up

♦ Tape

♦ 2 flyswatters (optional)

Objective

To reinforce vocabulary

Instructions

On the whiteboard or blackboard, tape up several visually represented vocabulary words. Divide the class into two teams. Ask one student from each team to come to the front of the class, giving them each a flyswatter if available. For fairness, make sure the students are the same distance from the board. Announce a vocabulary word. The first student to slap or swat the visual representation of the vocabulary word earns 1 point for the team. After their turn, these two students return to their seats and the next two students (one from each team) come to the front of the class. It is ideal if every student has an opportunity to compete.

Example

Our Spanish class played this game to review color vocabulary. We used sheets of construction paper for the visual representations. For example, I announces, "Green," and then both students attempted to swat the piece of green paper to earn a point for their team.

Notes

Some other vocabulary ideas for this game include clothing, weather, animals, transportation, physical characteristics (hair color, height, etc.), cultural symbols, house vocabulary (rooms in house, furniture, appliances, etc.), and any vocabulary that can be visually represented.

Baseball Review Game

Topic

♦ Review

Materials

♦ 3 chairs

♦ 3 paper baseball mitts (optional)

♦ 1 paper baseball bat (optional)

♦ Visual representations of vocabulary (optional)

Objective

To review target language material in an interactive, engaging format

Instructions

Write out a list of at least 20 review questions. The review questions function best when there is a one- or two-word answer. Divide the class into two teams and draw a baseball scoreboard on the board with team names and innings. One team is at bat first, and the other team is the basemen. Select three students from the basemen team to come to the front of the room and sit in the three chairs. The student in the first chair is first base, the student in the second chair is second base, and the student in the third chair is third base. Select one student from the batting team to come to the front of the room and stand behind the first baseman. The teacher asks a review question for the first baseman and the batter to attempt to answer. To make the game more visually stimulating while asking questions, use the board by drawing or writing numbers and incorporate visual representations of vocabulary such as clothing, objects, drawings of weather, or drawings of animals. When either student knows the answer to the question, they raise their hands to be called on. If the batter answers correctly first, he or she moves on to second base. If the baseman answers correctly first, however, the batter is out and must sit down. Moving on to second and third base and answering correctly before the each baseman earns the batter a run for the team. Just as in baseball, when the basemen team earns three outs, they become the batting team. Keep track of outs on the board for the basemen team for each half inning. Play as many innings as time available.

Index